GLOBETROTTER™

Travel Guide

CAPE
TOWN

PETER JOYCE

NEW
HOLLAND

NEW
HOLLAND

★★★ Highly recommended
★★ Recommended
★ See if you can

This edition first published in 2000
by New Holland Publishers (UK) Ltd
London • Cape Town • Sydney • Auckland
First published in 1999
10 9 8 7 6 5 4 3 2

24 Nutford Place
London W1H 6DQ
United Kingdom

80 McKenzie Street
Cape Town 8001
South Africa

14 Aquatic Drive
Frenchs Forest, NSW 2086
Australia

218 Lake Road
Northcote, Auckland
New Zealand

ISBN 1 85974 198 3

Manager Globetrotter Maps: John Loubser
Editor: Nune Jordaan
Editors (2nd edition): Sean Fraser, Gill Gordon
Design and DTP: Lyndall Hamilton
Cartography: Globetrotter Travel Maps

Reproduction by Hirt & Carter (Pty) Ltd, Cape Town
Printed and bound in Hong Kong by Sing Cheong
Printing Co. Ltd.

Although every effort has been made to ensure
accuracy of facts, telephone and fax numbers in this
book, the publishers will not be held responsible for
changes that occur at the time of going to press.

Photographic credits:
Africana Museum, page 13 (left); **Shaen Adey**,
pages 38 (bottom), 41 (top) 99, 112, 114, 115;
Captour, page 14; **Gerald Cubitt**, pages 4, 9, 13
(far right), 22, 23, 35, 38 (top), 39, 49 (bottom), 50,
55, 65, 77, 80 (bottom), 97, 98, 104; **Pat de la Harpe**,
101; **Roger de la Harpe**, pages 42 (bottom), 47 (left
and right), 51; **Leonard Hoffman** [SIL], pages 43, 60,
61, 88; **Walter Knirr**, pages 64, 102, 113; **Anne
Laing**, page 18; **Tertius Pickard** [Touchline Photo],
page 73; **Peter Pickford** [SIL], pages 44, 48, 67, 68,
81, 86; **Alain Proust**, pages 25 (top), 36 (bottom), 92;
Peter Ribton, page 49 (top); **Mark Skinner**, pages
26, 66; **Stans and Downing**, page 21; **Struik Image
Library** [SIL], pages 20, 21 (top) 29 (top), 70, 78, 93,
106; **Janek Szymanowski** [SIL], pages 31, 96;
Erhardt Thiel [SIL], cover, pages 7, 8, 10, 12, 15, 17,
25 (bottom), 29 (bottom), 30, 32, 33, 34, 36 (top), 40,
42 (top), 46, 52, 54 (top and bottom), 57 (top and
bottom), 62, 71, 72, 74 (top and bottom), 75, 76, 80
(top), 83, 84, 85, 89, 90 (bottom), 94, 110, 111; **Mark
van Aardt**, pages 11, 24, 37, 41 (bottom), 56, 58, 87
(left and right), 100; *Courtesy of* **V & A Waterfront
Company**, pages 19, 116; **Keith Young**, title page,
pages 53, 90 (top), 108, 109.

[SIL: Struik Image Library]

Cover: *Table Mountain with the 'tablecloth'.*
Title page: *Table Mountain floodlit.*

CONTENTS

1
Introducing
Cape Town

South Africa's 'Mother City', located at the southern tip of the continent, enjoys a matchless setting. Nestling snugly in the natural amphitheatre between the immensity of **Table Mountain** and the blue waters of **Table Bay**, it is a modern, cosmopolitan, stylishly attractive metropolis of graceful thoroughfares, handsome buildings and glittering shops – and it is fast becoming one of the southern hemisphere's premier tourist destinations.

Cape Town is a rather small city by world standards. The central area, its growth confined by both sea and mountain, covers just a dozen or so blocks. But the wider metropolitan area is enormous: the main thrust of development has been suburban, and the suburbs seem to go on for ever, each one a village or modest-sized town in its own right. To travel between, say, the western coastal centres of Kommetjie and Atlantis involves an 80km (50 miles) journey.

The city proper occupies the northern part of the **Cape Peninsula**, a 54km-long (34 miles), scenic finger of land that ends, dramatically, in the towering headland known as **Cape Point**. Popular belief has it that this is the division between the cold waters of the **Atlantic** and the warm waters of the **Indian Ocean** – a common misconception, since the technical separation takes places much further east, off the coast of **Cape Agulhas**, Africa's southernmost extremity. Nevertheless there are striking differences of character and mood between the Peninsula's flanking seas.

TOP ATTRACTIONS

*** Table Mountain: a world-famous landmark.
*** Cape Point: at the southern tip of the Peninsula; superb seascape vistas.
*** Victoria & Alfred Waterfront: historic dockland area transformed into a fantasia for the shopper, sightseer, diner and drinker.
*** Wine routes: in the lovely Constantia valley and vineyards of the hinterland.
*** The Castle: formidable, built to defend the colony.
** Beaches: white sands fringe the Peninsula's 150km (93 miles) shoreline.
** Scenic drives: along the coasts and Chapman's Peak.

Opposite: *The Mother City, nestled invitingly between mountain and bay.*

WILDLIFE HERITAGE

The Cape Peninsula, stretching from Signal Hill to Cape Point, and including Table Mountain, was declared a national park in May 1998. The new Cape Peninsula National Park covers approximately 30,000 hectares (74,000 acres) of both state and privately-owned land, and includes within its protectorate thousands of animal and plant species - including the *fynbos* of the unique Cape Floral Kingdom - making it eligible for status as a World Heritage Site.

Visitors expecting conventional images of the Dark Continent will be disappointed. There is nothing of the classical Africa about Cape Town and its surrounds – no heat-hazed veld stretching to far horizons, no distant drumbeats, no wild animals circling the bounds of your safari camp. The city is too old, and the region too well settled, and the countryside too green and gentle to sustain such romantic notions.

But there are other powerful attractions: a near-perfect Mediterranean climate, landscapes that delight the eye, spectacular beaches, the grandeur of **Table Mountain**, the exuberant **Waterfront** development, fine hotels, a myriad eating and drinking places, a lively and entertaining calendar of arts, and an enchanting wineland-and-mountain hinterland.

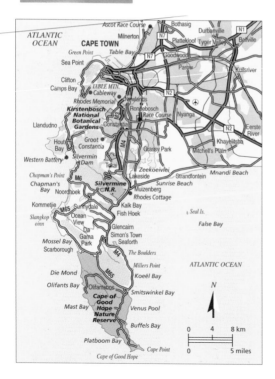

THE LAND

Much of the Peninsula comprises a well-watered, green-mantled sandstone plateau that reaches its most spectacular heights in the great bulk of **Table Mountain** itself. Two distinctively-shaped features; **Devil's Peak** and **Lion's Head**, stand sentry to either side of the massif. Defining the plateau's western rim is a series of imposing buttresses known as the **Twelve Apostles** (there are in fact 18 of them).

The shoreline is an entrancing combination of bay and white sand, high cliff and secluded cove. Inland are wooded valleys of magical beauty.

Left: *Strandfontein beach and, stretching into the horizon, the sandy plain known as the Cape Flats.*

INVADERS FROM OZ

Perhaps the most aggressive of the alien plants that endanger the Peninsula's unique indigenous flora is the **Port Jackson** willow, a hardy perennial tree that is native to **Australia**. These plants were brought in during the 1840s to stabilize the **Cape Flats** – the low, sandy area to the northeast of the city that the early Dutch settlers knew as *Die Groote Woeste Vlakte*, ('The Great Desolate Plain') for its nightmare of drifting dunes. The species adapted very well and it spread virulently over the wider region. It propagates quickly, and its hard, deep roots make clearing difficult and expensive.

To the north and east are the **Cape Flats**; a low, sandy flatland that once, not too long ago on the geophysical timetable, lay beneath the sea. Their shifting dunes proved a formidable obstacle to early Dutch colonists on their way inland, but the sands were eventually stabilized (with exotic vegetation that spread alarmingly, and today, threatens the region's indigenous flora) and are now heavily populated.

Beyond lie the hills, vineyards, orchards and lush pastures of the famed **Cape Winelands**.

Climate

Cape Town falls within the winter-rainfall belt, its climate **Mediterranean** in character. Weather patterns are complex and conditions variable – at times the city seems to pass through all four seasons in a single 24-hour period – but generally the summers are hot, sunny and very dry. The heat can be oppressive, especially when the warm 'berg wind' blows in from the interior. More often the air is cooled by a gusty, unnerving and sometimes violent (or 'black') southeaster that may reach gale force

CAPE TOWN	J	F	M	A	M	J	J	A	S	O	N	D
AVERAGE TEMP. °F	70	70	69	63	58	55	54	55	57	61	64	68
AVERAGE TEMP. °C	21	21	20	17	15	13	12	13	14	16	18	20
Hours of Sun Daily	11	10	9	7	6	6	6	7	8	9	10	11
SEA TEMP. °F	59	57	55	55	54	54	54	55	55	57	57	67
SEA TEMP. °C	15	14	13	13	12	12	12	13	13	14	14	14
RAINFALL in	1	1	1	2	3	4	3	3	2	2	1	1
RAINFALL mm	14	17	19	39	74	92	70	75	39	37	15	17
Days of Rainfall	5	4	5	8	12	12	11	13	10	8	5	5

Above: *A blustery start to the prestigious, biannual Cape-to-Rio yacht race. Cape Town features prominently on the international sailing calendar.*

LIVING FOSSILS

The **cycads** on view at **Kirstenbosch** are immensely ancient seed-bearing plants that date back more than 200 million years – to the time when the dinosaurs ruled the earth, and before the advent of flowering species. Though they look rather like palms, they are in fact relatives of the conifers. Two genera are indigenous to South Africa: *Encephalartos*, to which 28 species belong, and the single-species *Stangeria*. Cycads are strictly protected but, because of their rarity and high export value, remain vulnerable to illegal traders. Smugglers face stiff penalties.

---

and last for a week or even longer. The wind is commonly known as the **Cape Doctor** for its supposedly cleansing effect on the city (there may have been some truth in this in the early days when epidemic-type diseases were quite common at the Cape).

Winter is known as the **green season**. The moist, prevailing wind from the northwest brings damp chill and driving rain, and snow to the mountains of the coastal rampart. The long, cold, wet spells, though, are invariably broken by brief and delightfully unexpected intervals of warmth and welcome sunshine.

Cape Town is an attractive place to visit at any time of the year; each of the months has its appeal. Perhaps the best are those from high summer through to early winter (January to May), when the wind tends to keep its peace, the sun falls ever more kindly on the face, and the suburbs and countryside begin to take on the lovely, rustic colours of autumn.

Plant Life

The region's natural heritage is both unique and fascinating. Indigenous vegetation largely comprises the *fynbos* ('fine bush') of the **Cape Floral Kingdom**, a zone which extends over the southern coastal belt and contains about 8500 different species. Of these, some 2600 are found on the Peninsula itself.

The zone accounts for a minuscule 0.04% of the earth's land area and yet, because it is so rich in its floral diversity, it is ranked as one of the world's six major botanical divisions, enjoying equal status with the vast Boreal Kingdom encompassing the whole of North America and most of Europe and Asia.

Most of the plants are low-growing and hardy, well adapted to withstand the summertime droughts. Some are quite lovely; the more prominent include the **proteas**, more than 600 different kinds of **erica** (heath), the reed-like **restios**, the **lilies**, **orchids**, **red-hot pokers** and **disas**. An especially charming member of this last group is *Disa uniflora*, the 'Pride of Table Mountain'. The tallest of the family proteaceae is the **silver tree** (*Leucadendron argenteum*), which grows to more than 10m (33ft) and whose silver-green leaves, covered in silky-haired down, shimmer entrancingly in the breeze.

Around 80% of the different plant types are confined to particular areas of the Kingdom, some even to micro-habitats of just a few square metres, and this renders them especially vulnerable to human encroachment. It has been reckoned that more than 1500 species are threatened with extinction.

CITY PROFILE

Cape Town is the country's fourth largest urban centre and oldest city, founded in the mid-1600s to serve as a half-way station between Holland and its Far Eastern possessions. For centuries it was known as the **Tavern of the Seas**, drawing much of its prosperity from its harbour.

PROTEAS OF THE CAPE

The Western Cape is home to most of South Africa's 368 species of protea (indeed they are named after Proteus, a mythological Greek god who could change his shape at will). Among the best-known proteas are the **sugar-bush** (*Protea. repens*), the **waboom** (or wagon-tree, *Protea. nitida*), which grows to 7m (23ft), and the **king protea** (*Protea. cynaroides*), which has the largest and most attractive flowers of all the species and is South Africa's national flower.

FACTS AND FIGURES

● Cape Town harbour is the second biggest after Durban's; the dry-dock is the country's largest.
● The city lies at the south-western tip of the African continent, 1402km (871 miles) from Johannesburg in the north, 1753km (1089 miles) from Durban in the east, and 769km (478 miles) from Port Elizabeth along the southern coast.
● Total population is nearly four million.
● The highest point within the metropolitan area is Maclear's Beacon on Table Mountain, 1087m (3566ft) above sea level.

Left: *Adderley Street, the city's busiest thoroughfare.*

Maritime traffic has declined over the past few decades and the **harbour**, second in size only to Durban's, is a lot quieter than it was in the heydays of the great East Indiamen sailing ships and, later, the passenger steamers.

Still, Cape Town remains a major port city. **Ship repair** is a thriving industry; the dry-dock is the southern hemisphere's largest; mercantile enterprises contribute a lot to a local economy that also embraces **marine fisheries**, **petroleum refining**, light (and increasingly high-tech) **engineering**, **manufacturing** (notably clothing and textiles), **banking**, **insurance** and other services – and, of course, **tourism** is a rapidly expanding industry.

The metropolitan area extends southwards, along the suburban railway line, through Observatory, Mowbray, Rondebosch, Newlands, Wynberg (these are the oldest of the suburbs, founded as colonial farms in the 17th century) to the historic naval centre of Simon's Town, near Cape Point. The fashionable western or 'Atlantic' suburbs (Green Point, Sea Point, Clifton, Camps Bay) are concentrated closer to the city; affluent and semi-rural Constantia occupies much of the central Peninsula.

The northern and eastern, or Cape Flats, areas are dense with industrial and middle and lower-income residential development. Among much else they encompass Bellville, which has a population exceeding 100,000 and gained city status in the 1970s; the fairly new town of Mitchell's Plain; great swathes of high-density housing (including the townships of Langa, Nyanga, Gugulethu and the relatively young Khayelitsha).

THE CRUEL SEA

Over the centuries more than 1300 ships have been wrecked along South Africa's rocky coasts, many of them off the 'Cape of Storms'. In the great gale of 1865 no less than 11 vessels sank in Table Bay alone. Numerous others foundered on or close to the coasts (**Shipwreck and Lighthouse Route**; details from Captour). Among the many sea-related tales of tragedy and heroism is that of Wolraad Woltemade, who braved the ocean seven times to rescue survivors from *De Jonge Thomas*, wrecked in the bay in June 1773. On the eighth trip, both he and his horse disappeared beneath the waves. The Woltemade Decoration has ranked as South Africa's highest civilian honour for gallantry.

HISTORY IN BRIEF

Cape Town was born on 6 April 1652 when Commander Jan van Riebeeck led his small party of Dutch settlers ashore to establish a replenishment station for the Indies-bound trading fleets of the **Dutch East India Company's** great maritime empire.

At that time, and for generations before, the Peninsula was home to groups of **Khoikhoi** (Hottentots), semi-nomadic, cattle-owning people related to the **San** (Bushmen), hunter-gatherers of the interior.

Van Riebeeck's instructions were to cultivate friendly relations with the local inhabitants – to whom, after all, the countryside belonged. The colonists needed fresh meat, the Khoikhoi were keen to barter, and for the most part the two cultures managed to coexist in reasonable harmony. Later, rivalry for grazing land and trading rights was to lead to open conflict.

The Early Years

The settlers were determined to make their outpost self-sufficient. Their prime tasks were 'to erect defences, and to secure herbs, flesh, water and other needful refreshments'.

Within days of landing Van Riebeeck had marked out the site of a fort, and before the end of April the first walls were up and supporting five cannons. There were plenty of setbacks – the Cape rainstorms played havoc with the earthen ramparts – but the structure served its purpose well enough for 20-odd years. In due course it was to be replaced by a splendid, new five-sided bastion known as **The Castle**, today South Africa's oldest occupied building. After an initial struggle with the elements, the newcomers also established the **Company's Garden**;

> **THE EARLIEST EXPLORERS**
>
> 15th-century Portuguese navigators were not the first to see Africa's southern-most shores. 2000 years earlier, Phoenician galleys almost certainly rounded the Cape, although unlike later voyagers they sailed down the east coast. They had been sent by the pharaoh, Necho, to pass Zanzibar and return 'through the Pillars of Hercules' (Gibraltar). According to Greek historian Herodotus, the Phoenicians reported that, in sailing around Libya (the ancient name for Africa), they 'had the sun on their right hand'. So, they had travelled west-wards past Cape Point!

Opposite: *The harbour is among the southern hemi-sphere's biggest.*
Below: *The Castle of Good Hope is the most enduring of the buildings erected by early European settlers.*

SLAVERY AT THE CAPE

The first **Cape** slaves arrived in 1657, from **Angola** and **West Africa**. Later, they were brought in from the **Dutch** possessions of the **Indies**. Those assigned to work in town were rather better off than their country cousins: they were lodged in the slave quarters (now the Cultural History Museum), and provided with regular meals and schooling for their children. Some skilled slaves, who could hire themselves out as artisans, earned enough to buy their freedom. In 1710 there were about 1200 adult slaves in the Dutch colony. By the end of the century, the figure had risen to 17,000 – which was more than the white population of the period. Slavery was finally abolished in 1834 by Act of Parliament.

Below: *The historic South African Museum flanking the Company's Garden.*

a flourishing vegetable farm, now public gardens. Over the years its rows of humble plants gave way to more decorative features – lemon and fruit trees, an avenue of oaks, a pleasure lodge (now **De Tuynhuys**: the President's city office), a slave lodge (today the **Cultural History Museum**; *see* p. 30), a menagerie (now an aviary), and an area set aside for the cultivation of rare plants – a role the garden still fulfils with honour. Today they are much smaller than they were – grand buildings have encroached on three sides – but remain as lovely as ever.

During the first years, other basics of civic life made their appearance: hospital, jetty, simple houses, a scatter of public buildings. Most imposing of the latter was the high-steepled, thatched and gabled **Groote Kerk**, the Dutch Reformed (Calvinist) mother church, erected in 1704. Linking the shoreline – which at that time ran through what is now the city centre – with the Company's Garden was the elegant, stone-paved, oak-lined **Heerengracht** (translating roughly as 'Gentlemen's walk along the canal'), renamed **Adderley Street** during the late 19th century. The section below the fountain currently named the Heerengracht, is part of the land (Foreshore) that was reclaimed from the sea in the 1930s.

Other prominent features of early 18th-century Cape Town included a spacious **Grand Parade** flanking the Castle; Greenmarket Square, the town's commercial hub, and some fine private homes built in the evolving and increasingly beautiful Cape Dutch style. Special among the latter was **Koopmans-De Wet House** on Strand Street. By the time the British displaced the Dutch at the end of the 18th century, Cape Town had grown into an elegant little place, one of the

Left: *Charming Adderley Street in the 1830s.*
Above: *Harvesting Cape wines, which are fast gaining worldwide recognition.*

southern hemisphere's busiest ports and host to ships and sailors from a dozen nations. Its population comprised about 6000 Europeans and several thousand more people of Malay and mixed-descent stock, many of them slaves or descendants of slaves. Suburbs had crept up the lower slopes of Table Mountain, and a chain of rural centres, leading from nearby Woodstock to Simon's Town, had gone a long way towards taming the Peninsula.

Spirit of the Vine

From the earliest years the settlers began importing much-needed labour for a settlement that was expanding, not only through the Peninsula but into the hinterland.

Prompted by the need to feed the colony, men had been released from Company employment to establish farms, and during the 1660s they began infiltrating the traditional Khoikhoi lands of the interior. **Stellenbosch**, 48km (30 miles) northeast of Cape Town, was founded in 1679 and thereafter valley after valley was occupied, the countryside turned over to pasture, wheat and the growing of wine grapes.

In fact the first vines had been planted by Van Riebeeck himself in 1655, to yield 'mainly muscadel and other white round grapes of truly fine bouquet and taste'. The long-serving (1679-99) and able Governor

---

THE FIRST VINTAGE

The Western Cape's flourishing **wine industry** has its origins in the very first year of white settlement. Just a month after stepping ashore in April 1652, **Jan van Riebeeck** asked his masters in Amsterdam for 'vines which ought to thrive as well on these hill slopes as they do in Spain and France'. In due course 12,000 were growing on his private farm, and in 1659 he was able to confide to his journal that 'today, praise be to God, wine can be made for the first time from Cape grapes, namely from the new must fresh from the vat'. Well before the end of the century grapes were being harvested around the young country towns of **Stellenbosch**, **Franschhoek** and **Paarl**.

Simon van der Stel also showed a very keen interest in **viticulture**, devoting some of his boundless energy and part of his gracious **Groot Constantia** property, south of Table Mountain, to vineyards. The excellent Constantia wines were eventually to find their way onto the aristocratic tables of Europe.

The arrival in 1688 of a small group of **French Huguenots** – Protestant refugees from Europe's religious wars – gave impetus to the fledgling industry. By 1690 half a million vines were flourishing on the Peninsula and in the winelands around Stellenbosch.

The British Occupation

For more than two centuries Cape Town functioned as the centre of a growing colony that, under the Dutch, pushed its frontiers 800km (500 miles) eastwards, through the lands of the Xhosa as far as the Great Fish River.

With the decline of the Netherlands towards the end of the 18th century, the British first took control of the Cape in 1795, and some time later withdrew from the colony for about eight years. They returned, however, in 1806 and the territory became a **Crown Colony** in 1814, progressing first to representative government (1854) and finally to full self-government (1872) with a constitution modelled on the two-chamber Westminster system. The vote was based on income and property rather than on race – a concession to democracy that the apartheid politicians later withdrew. A high commissioner was appointed to look after British interests and, with **Union** in 1910, the colony became one of the country's four provinces, with Cape Town designated the nation's legislative capital.

Below: *A rare plate bearing the monogram of the Dutch East India Company.*
Opposite: *The Mount Nelson Hotel, gracious host to a who's-who of notables for the past century.*

Growing Up

Around the middle of the 1800s Cape Town's population stood at a modest 24,000, but the latter half of the century brought rapid growth, fuelled by revenue from the fabulous **Kimberley** diamond fields far to the north and from the city's ever-busier harbour.

The first tarred road was laid in the 1850s (timber paving had previously been tried, but proved too slippery), as was the inaugural railway line – between **Adderley Street** and the Winelands' town of **Wellington**. The original locomotive, built in 1859 in Scotland and shipped out for assembly, is on view in the main station concourse. Horse-drawn trams were introduced in 1863, initially operating between the city and the ocean suburb of **Sea Point**. The first motor car took to the streets in 1895, and a year later the electric tram heralded the demise of the horse as Cape Town's principal means of transport.

By the end of the century the central area had developed beyond recognition, and Cape Town had acquired its own, unique character as the 'gateway to Africa'. Ships' chandlers did a roaring trade, **Union Castle** mail-ships regularly offloaded cargoes of immigrants, seamen from a score of far-flung lands haunted the taverns and lodging houses, and attractive hotels catered for the more well-to-do visitors.

Among these was the grand new **Mount Nelson Hotel**, which hosted a veritable who's-who of Britain during the **Anglo-Boer War** (1899-1902), including a young, dashing Winston Churchill, of London's *Morning Post*.

The city was equally hospitable during **World War II**, when it welcomed troopships bound for the Far East theatre.

PICK OF THE MUSEUMS

*** The Castle, Buitenkant Street: oldest occupied building in the country. Period furniture, paintings, militaria. Cultural Studies Centre.
*** The Cultural History Museum, Adderley Street: postal relics, ceramics, weaponry, coins.
*** Groot Constantia, Constantia Valley: Cape Dutch mansion, interesting wine museum, cellar tours.
** South African Museum, Queen Victoria Street: geology, archeology, natural history.
** Koopmans-De Wet House, Strand Street: an elegant Cape historic home and a showcase of the arts.
* The Old Synagogue, Government Avenue: treasures of the Jewish Museum.
* Simon's Town Museum, Peninsula east coast: naval history and much else.
* Rugby Museum, in Newlands: world's largest.

HISTORICAL CALENDAR

Pre-colonial era Cape Peninsula and hinterland occupied by groups of Khoikhoi (Hottentots), semi-nomadic, cattle-owning people who over the centuries had competed with and largely displaced aboriginal San (Bushmen) hunter-gatherers as the region's dominant human presence.

1460-1510 The age of Portuguese exploration: navigators progressively chart sea route to India. Dias rounds Cape in 1488; Da Gama reaches India in 1498; De Saldanha sails into Table Bay and climbs Table Mountain in 1503; D'Almeida killed in battle with Khoikhoi in 1510, after which the Portuguese lose interest.

1580 English admiral Drake sights 'the fairest Cape in all the circumference of the earth'.

1595-1647 Dutch East India Company fleets explore coast, trade with Khoikhoi.

1652 Dutch party under Jan van Riebeeck establishes Cape settlement.

1657 First white farmers settle the land. First slaves imported.

1659 First serious conflict between Khoikhoi and white colonists. First wine produced.

1660s Explorers make their way inland, and along south and west coasts.

1671 Second settler-Khoikhoi war.

1679 Castle of Good Hope completed. The enlightened Simon van der Stel appointed Cape commander (later governor); Stellenbosch founded.

1685 Slaves granted right to buy their freedom.

1713 First great smallpox epidemic devastates Khoikhoi community; other epidemics follow in 1755 and 1767.

1780-83 War between Holland and Britain hastens demise of Dutch East India Co, in decline since 1750s. Cape Town hosts French troops (Holland's allies).

1795-1803 First British occupation of the Cape.

1798 Much of Cape Town destroyed by fire.

1803 Cape reverts to Dutch rule.

1806 Second British occupation.

1814 Cape formally ceded to Britain.

1829 South African College (now University of Cape Town) founded.

1834 Slavery abolished.

1859-60 Work starts on first railway line (to Wellington) and on Table Bay docks.

1869 Kimberley diamonds discovered; Cape Town enters new age of growth and prosperity.

1872 Cape Colony gains responsible government.

1879 Cape Town and London linked by cable.

1881 First electric lighting installed.

1890 Cecil Rhodes becomes Cape premier.

1892 Cape Town to Johannesburg railway line officially inaugurated.

1899-1902 Anglo-Boer War; Cape Town accommodates British forces.

1910 Cape Town becomes legislative capital of unified South Africa.

1918 Influenza epidemic kills thousands.

1925 Prince of Wales visits city.

1926 First motor-powered mailship arrives at Table Bay.

1939-45 City welcomes Allied troops.

1947 British royal family visits Cape Town.

1956 The Coloured people of the country lose their parliamentary vote.

1957 The British Royal Navy relinquishes Simon's Town naval base.

1960 British premier Macmillan delivers 'wind of change' address to parliament in Cape Town.

1963 Nelson Mandela imprisoned 'for life'.

1966 District Six declared a 'white' area; removal of Coloured residents begins. South African prime minister Verwoerd assassinated by deranged parliamentary messenger.

1967 Christiaan Barnard performs world's first heart transplant at Groote Schuur Hospital.

1970s and 1980s Liberation struggle gains momentum; mounting unrest in townships.

1990 Mandela released from prison; addresses huge crowd on Grand Parade.

1994 First democratic elections. President Nelson Mandela opens historic parliament in Cape Town.

Today Cape Town is of course much bigger and – because the apartheid years brought so much human deprivation and suffering – less complacent, more socially and economically unstable. But the core personality and charm with which it has become associated, remains. The Mother City is still very much in the hospitality business, beckoning the traveller, entertaining him well, and sending him on his way with pleasant memories.

MUSIC OF THE STREETS

The **Cape Coloured** community has a lively musical tradition, drawn from a rich cultural heritage. Although the origins of many of the *ghomma*-style songs are obscure, the cheerful and sometimes racy words and melodies are still heard at gatherings. The **Minstrel Carnival** is a wonderfully animated New Year street festival of music and dance that owes much to the early African-American minstrel troupes. On this annual occasion, brightly costumed bands mass together on the **Grand Parade** before making their way along the thoroughfares to **Green Point**.

THE PEOPLE

Greater Cape Town's population totals well over three million, a figure that will rise by another million and more within the next decade if the present pattern of 'urban drift' continues.

Ethnic origins cover the racial and cultural spectrum, from old and mostly affluent **Dutch**, **Cape-Afrikaner** and **English-Colonial** families to penniless, destitute shack-dwellers recently arrived from rural Transkei. The area was previously an 'independent homeland' but is now incorporated into the newly-established province of the Eastern Cape.

Largest of the 'groups' – a much looser term now than in the bad old days of segregation – is the mixed-descent or **Coloured**, a society with diverse roots. It is largely Afrikaans-speaking (though most of its members are fluent in English, spoken with a lilting accent), largely Christian and wholly Westernized in lifestyle and custom. It does, however, have a distinctive and joyous musical tradition. On New Year's Day sections of the community put on the Minstrel Carnival, an exuberant and marvellously colourful parade through the city's streets.

POPULATION BREAKDOWN OF THE WESTERN CAPE

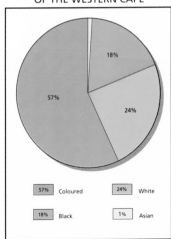

18%
57%
24%

| 57% | Coloured | 24% | White |
| 18% | Black | 1% | Asian |

THE SWORD DANCE

Among the more dramatic of **Cape Muslim** traditions is the *Ratiep*, a sword dance, led by a 'master of ceremonies' (*Khalifa*). It was performed under a self-induced trance during which young men pierced their flesh with swords and other sharp instruments. Remarkably, this did not draw blood, and left no wound. Today the ritual has lost its religious relevance and in fact many of the *imams* (spiritual leaders), frown on the practice, though it still takes place as an occasional spectacle.

The Coloured people were a more-or-less integrated part of Cape society until the 1950s when, after some cynical tampering with the constitution, the government removed their voting rights. A decade later many also lost their homes: the renowned District Six inner suburb was demolished and its residents moved to the bleakness of the Cape Flats (*see* p. 35).

A prominent subgroup are the 200,000 **Cape Muslims**, whose forefathers came, as slaves, from the Indonesian islands and other eastern regions. They were valued for their skills as craftsmen (and for their wonderful cuisine; *see* p. 20). Many who were not originally of the faith converted to Islam on arrival. Among the newcomers were high-born political exiles – men such as Sheik Yusuf, who had led a rebellion against the Dutch in Java.

With the abolition of slavery in the 1830s, a fair number of these highly-respected people settled in the picturesque Bo-Kaap ('Upper Cape Town', also known as the Malay Quarter) on the slopes of Signal Hill, on the city's western perimeter. There was little intermarriage with other groups, and it has remained a highly integrated, devout community. Its members attend their city mosques, and many make pilgrimages, not only to Mecca (as is required of all Muslims who can afford the journey) but to the local *kramats*, or tombs of the holy men. Among the more eye-catching of ancient traditions to survive is the *Ratiep*, a trance-induced sword dance that once played a part in religious ceremony. It is still sometimes performed in the Cape.

The majority of Cape Town's black citizens are migrants or the descendants of migrants from the historic **Xhosa** 'homelands' of the Eastern Cape. Most live on the Cape Flats, in the sprawling suburbs of Langa, Nyanga, Gugulethu and Khayelitsha and the surrounding informal settlements; many in appalling conditions.

The black people of the region have inherited a harsh legacy. Under the apartheid regime the

Opposite: *Happy faces sporting the new South African flag in celebration of the 1995 Rugby World Cup victory.*
Left: *Inside one of the Waterfront's restaurants. The leisure area, comprising the old harbour's Victoria and Alfred docks, is a glittering, and rapidly growing, tourist mecca.*

southwestern Cape was deemed a 'Coloured preference area', and if you were a black person you couldn't get a job or a place to live, and you faced repatriation.

Forced removals did not halt the influx. Poor people continued to pour in from a countryside that could no longer meet their minimum needs. And because they were 'illegal', very little provision was made for them in the way of houses, schools, clinics, roads and services.

South Africa is now a democratic country, movement is no longer restricted, and a lot of money is being invested in upliftment. But huge backlogs remain in the Cape and elsewhere, and these issues definitely pose the greatest challenge of the future.

Food and Drink
Cape Town's myriad restaurants offer the full range of food styles – from the classic to the exotic. Areas with especially heavy concentrations of eateries are Sea Point, whose Main Road is known as the 'Culinary Mile', the Victoria and Alfred Waterfront, and the southern suburban stretch from Rondebosch through to Claremont.

The local **line-fish**, **rock lobster** (crayfish) and **abalone** (*perlemoen*) are usually excellent, though the **shellfish** tends to be expensive. Antelope **venison** (including springbok pie) is something of a speciality, and **ostrich** steaks are an increasingly popular menu item.

TAVERN TAPESTRY

Cape Town is well served by pubs. Most offer a simple lunchtime menu – ploughman's platter, fish and chips, pies, liver and onions, pork and lamb chops, casseroles, with vegetables and salads – at reasonable prices. Some also feature live music. The city's oldest pub is **The Perseverance Tavern** in Buitenkant Street. **The Crowbar**, in Waterkant Street, is very English in character and clientele. **Foresters Arms** (Newlands) and **The Heidelberg** and **The River Club**, (both in Observatory) are of the German beer-garden type. The bistros and coffee shops on St George's Mall are popular lunchtime venues. **The Rockin' Shamrock** in Loop Street has a lively Irish atmosphere. Leading Waterfront pubs include **Ferryman's**, **Quay Four**, **The Sports Café** and the **Hard Rock Café.**

Old Cape **country fare**, available in selected restaurants, evolved among the rural Afrikaner communities. Common ingredients of the meal include tender Karoo lamb, sweet potatoes, cinnamon-flavoured pumpkin, sweetcorn fritters and, for dessert: milk tart, *koeksisters* and a selection of sticky preserves known as *konfyt*, all washed down with fragrant *rooibos* tea; made from the leaves of an indigenous herbal bush.

TABLE TALK	
Biltong: Air-dried spiced meat.	**Melktert**: or 'Milk tart'. Cinnamon-coated baked custard on a thin, pastry base.
Bobotie: Curried meat-loaf topped with savoury custard.	
Boerewors: Spicy, coriander-flavoured 'farmer's sausage'.	**Mielie**: Sweetcorn; corn-on-the-cob.
Braai: 'braaivleis', a barbecue.	**Pap**: Maize-meal.
Bredie: Fragrant stew, with potatoes, onions and sometimes vegetables.	**Perlemoen**: Abalone.
	Potjiekos: Slow-simmering stew usually cooked over an open fire in a large three-legged pot.
Crayfish: Rock lobster.	
Koeksister: Either cumin-flavoured oval of plaited-dough coated with coconut or a deep-fried dough 'twist' soaked in syrup.	**Snoek**: A firm-fleshed, strongly-flavoured fish, good for smoking and braaing.
	Sosatie: A skewer of curry-marinated meat.
Konfyt: Sweet preserves.	

Rather tastier and less stodgy is **Malay cuisine**, introduced by the early slaves from Indonesia and famed for its aromatic *boboties* (curried meatloaf topped with savoury custard), *bredies* (fragrant stews, usually of mutton, potatoes and vegetables, although *waterblommetjie bredie* is a piquant variety made from a type of indigenous waterlilies), spicy *samoosas* and gooey desserts. The traditional style has been refined over the centuries, taking on elements of early Dutch, French Huguenot and Indian cooking.

Outdoor entertainment in Cape Town invariably centres around the *braai* or *braaivleis*; a standard barbecue of long-marinated lamb, venison, beef, chicken, spicy

boerewors ('farmer's sausage'), potatoes baked in foil and salads. The men invariably do the cooking, which is considered something of an art form. Charcoal, wood or both are used for fuel, the wood imparting a distinctive and tasty flavour to the food.

Also popular is *potjiekos*; a flavourful stew cooked gently for hours and even days in a giant cast-iron pot over an open fire.

Opposite: *A traditional Cape Malay feast.*
Left: *Typical Cape fare – kebabs, 'potjie' and 'pap'.*
Below: *The Nico Theatre Centre, focal point of the city's performing arts.*

Traditional **African cuisine** does not yet appear on many menus, but this is changing, as innovative chefs introduce elements of African cuisine to their dishes. For most black people, eating remains a practical necessity; the ordinary meal of the day in the townships tends to be a no-nonsense affair in which maize-meal (*pap*), boiled meat or cabbage, or *samp* and beans is the order of the day. But living standards are improving.

There are some 4000 locally produced **wines** on the market, from delicate dry whites to full-bodied reds. All are drinkable, many are noteworthy, a few truly memorable and the better ones are fast gaining an international reputation. The best way to explore the range is to embark on one or more of the world-famous wine routes (*see* p. 79). Bookshops and some liquor stores stock informative guides to the wine-growing areas and the many labels on offer.

Entertainment and the Arts
Theatre and **music** are alive and doing well in Cape Town. The grander shows – drama, opera, ballet, oratorio and the occasional lavish musical – are staged at the **Nico Theatre Centre** (D.F. Malan Street, Foreshore), mostly under the auspices of the **Cape Performing Arts Board** (Capab), but an increasing number of international acts are also performed in the three auditoria.

Popular plays, music and, sometimes, local and experimental drama can be enjoyed at the **Baxter Theatre Complex** (on Main Road, Rondebosch), whose two main halls each have a 600-plus capacity. There's also a small studio/workshop.

Some excellent professional productions - especially light musical and comic fare - are staged in Camps Bay's recently revamped **Theatre on the Bay.** There are also a number of smaller, intimate theatres: check the local press for up-to-date details.

The Cape Town Philharmonic Orchestra caters for most tastes in classical music; evening concerts are occasionally performed in ornately Baroque surrounds at the **City Hall**, which may also host Sunday evening performances during the winter months.

In summer, Sunday evening concerts may be held at the Victoria and Alfred Waterfront's open-air **Agfa Amphitheatre**.

There's plenty of live entertainment – jazz, pop, cabaret – on the night-time scene. Venues and performers change all the time; consult the local newspapers, Captour or Leisure and Entertainment Guides which are available from major bookshops. Most of the bigger hotels also offer dinner-dancing.

SUN, SEA AND SAND

Bloubergstrand, north of the city, offers safe bathing and fine views of Table Mountain. **Milnerton** has 8km (5 miles) of white sand and a big lagoon.
The long stretch of the Peninsula west coast between **Sea Point** and **Camps Bay**, known as the 'Cape Riviera', is especially attractive. **Clifton** has four fashionable beaches. Also close-by are **Maiden's Cove** (for skin-diving), **Glen Beach** (for surfing) and **Camps Bay** (for sunbathing). **Llandudno** is scenically beautiful; **Sandy Bay** is for all-over tanning. **The Cape of Good Hope Nature Reserve** has several pleasant and safe spots; **Maclear** beach is excellent for scuba-diving and bathing. **Muizenberg** on the Peninsula east coast has a long and beautiful beach. **St James** (sheltered, tidal pool) and **Boulders** (safe bathing, penguin sanctuary).

Sport and Recreation

There are some exquisite **beaches** along the Peninsula's shoreline and up the coast towards Bloubergstrand. Those on the western or 'Atlantic' side are sheltered from the prevailing summer wind but the sea is rather cold for comfortable bathing. On the other hand, False Bay in the east tends to be breezy but water temperatures are about 5°C warmer and reach about 23°C in summer. Visitors should stick to popular areas – those monitored by beach constables and life savers – rather than seek seclusion.

You'll find especially attractive stretches of beach at Clifton and next-door Camps Bay, close to town, and at Muizenberg on the east coast. Noordhoek, in the west, is ideal for an early-morning **horseback ride**.

The rockier coves beckon the **snorkeller** and **scuba-diver**. There are strict limits for rock lobster and abalone catches. **Sea angling** is virtually unrestricted; rock and surf fishermen reel in *snoek* (barracouta), steenbras, red roman and *kabeljou* (kob); game fishing enthusiasts take marlin, swordfish and three species of tunny (tuna). A number of companies offer **game-fishing** charters.

Opposite: *Much of the Cape Peninsula is beautifully wooded which is ideal countryside for rambles, walks and hikes.*

Above: *The white sands of Clifton's popular and fashionable Fourth Beach.*

Because the sea is easily accessible from almost anywhere in the Peninsula, opportunities for **yachting, power-boating, board-sailing, waterskiing, parasailing** and other aquatic sports are limitless. For those who prefer more structured **swimming**, public pools are located in Sea Point (seawater), in the city at the top of Long Street (indoor, heated), and in Newlands (Olympic-size); and smaller municipal pools in the suburbs.

The Peninsula is fine **walking** country; prime areas are the more secluded stretches of coastline, the hills and valleys inland, and, of course, the slopes of Table Mountain itself. There are five excellent walking routes up Table Mountain (*see* p.41).

Cape Town is one of the few South African cities whose central area is best explored on foot – much of what there is to see is within easy strolling distance. A word of caution: South Africa has been undergoing something of a social upheaval, poverty is everywhere and free-spending tourists are vulnerable to street crime. The city's main thoroughfares and open spaces are safe enough in busy daylight hours and there are helpful policemen about; at other times it's wise to take your urban ramble in a group.

Right: *Among the country's leading health resorts is the High Rustenberg Hydro, near Stellenbosch.*
Opposite: *Sea Point promenade is popular among joggers and poeple who walk their dogs.*
Opposite below: *Bowling beneath the grandeur of the Table Mountain range.*

BEST WALKS

*** City centre and **Waterfront:** historical routes; booklets available from Captour.
*** Table Mountain: offers numerous walks and climbs; excellent guidebooks available at bookshops.
*** Cape of Good Hope Nature Reserve: there are many short or long trails.
*** Kirstenbosch National Botanical Gardens: for the lover of plants and scenic splendour. Very relaxing.
** Hout Bay: several routes through beautiful hiking and rambling countryside.
** Cecilia forest: fringing the enchanting Constantia Valley. Easy walks.
** Silvermine Nature Reserve: an unspoiled wilderness. Excellent views.
* Tokai forest: six charted trails, two hour walk to Elephant's Eye cave, also called Prinseskasteel.
* Newlands forest: for either a ramble through the pine trees or a walk up to the saddle linking Devil's Peak with Table Mountain.

In the countryside, stick to well-worn paths and recommended walking routes.

Cycling is an exhilarating way of exploring the region. The local pedal-power association organizes weekend excursions and fun rides throughout the year. The annual Argus/Pick 'n Pay Cycle Tour, a challenging 105km (65 miles) around the Peninsula, is held in March and attracts about 24,000 entrants. Participants, however, must register well in advance to avoid disappointment.

Golf and **bowling** clubs welcome guests; courses and greens are of a high standard.

There are also several well equipped and efficiently run **health studios** and clinics in the metropolitan area, some of which are part of hotels. The exclusive High Rustenberg Hydro resort, in Ida's Valley near Stellenbosch, caters for health-seeking visitors. A health and spa guide is available from Captour.

More than 300 species of birds have been identified in the wider Cape Town area, including sugarbirds, paradise flycatchers, black eagles that ride the high thermals and a variety of aquatic birds. Bird-watchers have a wide choice of venues. In the city centre is the Company's Garden, and in Newlands: Kirstenbosch National Botanical Gardens. To the north of the city is Milnerton lagoon and the Rietvlei Conservation Area – a major waterfowl breeding reserve, home to the Caspian and

FOR THE GOLFER

Visitors to the city are welcome at the Peninsula's
many golf clubs and on the
splendid courses of the
Winelands to the north and
east. The Captour information office at the Tourism
Gateway will provide particu-
lars on the most popular golf
courses, including Mowbray
Golf Club, Rondebosch Golf
Club, the Metropolitan in
Mouille Point, Westlake in
Lakeside, Clovelly Golf Club
and the Royal Cape Golf
Club in Wynberg. Driving
ranges are located in Stik-
land, Durbanville, Maitland
and at the River Club in
Mowbray. Alternatively, avid
golfers may contact the
**Western Province Golf
Union** directly, tel: (021)
686-1668, fax: 686-5633.

Arctic tern, the fish eagle and flamingo – and a haven for
contaminated or injured seabirds, particularly penguins.

Rondevlei Nature Reserve, a shallow lake surrounded
by coastal dunes near the shores of False Bay, is sanctuary for an even more prolific bird life – 225 species in all.
There are two lookout towers with telescopes and five
hides to facilitate **bird-watching**, (the reserve also has
four hippos). Another rewarding spot is the extensive
Cape of Good Hope Nature Reserve (*see* p. 59), which
covers the southern tip of the Peninsula.

Organized Sport

Major provincial and international **rugby** and **cricket**
matches are played at the famed Newlands stadiums, in
the leafy southern suburbs 7km (4.5 miles) from the centre of the city. **Road running** is a popular pastime and
quite competitive, the major event being the Two Oceans
marathon, held over Easter each year (12,000-plus
entrants). **Athletics** and **soccer** also enjoy wide support.

Apart from the Norwich grounds in Newlands, sports
amenities generally fall short of standards in more developed countries. Facilities in
high-density townships are especially lamentable. When Cape Town was nominated to
host the 2004 Olympic Games (which went to Athens), many new proposals were insti-
tuted for upgrading facilities and government is encouraging private sponsors to continue with their plans to invest in new infrastructure for world-class sporting events.

2
City and Mountain

Cape Town's most prominent thoroughfare is the old Heerengracht, laid out in the city's infancy. It runs straight as an arrow from the harbour, south towards the majesty of **Table Mountain**. The original route twice changes its name (the result of later decisions) – first to Adderley Street and then to Government Avenue, which passes through the exquisite **Company's Garden**. **Adderley Street** is the city's commercial heartland and the point from which, if you're on an exploratory walkabout, you should perhaps start: you'll get your bearings here, and much of what the city centre has to offer is within walking distance. The **Tourism Gateway**, the city's official tourism and information station, is at the junction of the Heerengracht and Adderley Street, east of the fountain, and houses all the visitors' information offices, including Captour (local interest), Satour (national interest) and private tour operators.

By African standards, this is an old city, and much from the early days remains, visible in the museums of course, but also in buildings that have survived centuries of change. Most time-honoured of these is the massive **Castle** that once guarded Cape Town against sea approaches, while among the most attractive are those erected in the later 18th century, many of them designed by the talented twosome: architect Louis Thibault and sculptor Anton Anreith. Later decades also produced their gems, notably the charmingly filigreed, wrought-iron legacies of the Victorian era that decorate **Long Street** and its neighbours.

MYTHS OF THE MOUNTAIN

The spirit of **Adamaster**, the mythical giant who tried and failed to overthrow the gods of ancient Greece, is ever-present on Table Mountain. Dutchman **Jan van Hunks** challenged the Devil to a pipe-smoking contest – hence the mountain's billowing clouds. **Antje Somers**, a crook who dresses as a woman and lurks on the slopes to rob those who stray from the paths.

Opposite: *The Old Town House on Greenmarket Square. Umbrellas shade the busy street-traders.*

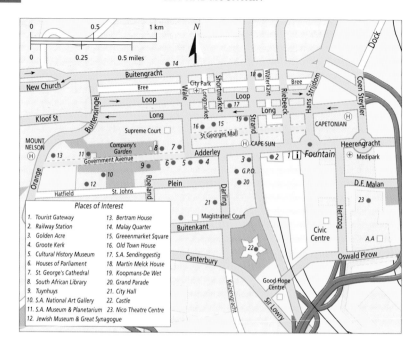

0 0.5 1 km N	
0 0.25 0.5 miles	

Places of Interest

1. Tourist Gateway
2. Railway Station
3. Golden Acre
4. Groote Kerk
5. Cultural History Museum
6. Houses of Parliament
7. St. George's Cathedral
8. South African Library
9. Tuynhuys
10. S.A. National Art Gallery
11. S.A. Museum & Planetarium
12. Jewish Museum & Great Synagogue
13. Bertram House
14. Malay Quarter
15. Greeenmarket Square
16. Old Town House
17. S.A. Sendinggestig
18. Martin Melck House
19. Koopmans-De Wet
20. Grand Parade
21. City Hall
22. Castle
23. Nico Theatre Centre

THE FORESHORE

This flat, 145-hectare (358 acres) part of the northern city was reclaimed from the sea in the 1930s and 1940s. Great quantities of sand and silt were dredged up and dumped on the landward side, covering for ever the old harbour, its fine promenade and a beach that was invariably cluttered with rowing boats and oars, tackle boxes, ropes and stone anchors. Local writer Lawrence Green nostalgically recalled that, around the turn of the century, it was a memorable sight when the fishing fleet put out under spritsails, and an even more vivid one when it returned, for then 'all the old Malay priests and grey-bearded *hadjis*, all the bright-skirted womenfolk and *fezzed* small boys seemed to be waiting on the sand ...'.

The area is now bisected by the broad reaches of the **Heerengracht**, notable for its handsome flanking office blocks, its shops, and its central island of lawns, palms and fountains. There are statues of Portuguese navigator Bartolomeu Dias who rounded the Cape in 1488, founder Jan van Riebeeck and his wife Maria de la Queillerie, and at the bottom of Adderley Street, the **War Memorial**.

If you walk east along **Hertzog Boulevard** (but don't do so when the southeaster is blowing: it's little short of a wind tunnel) you'll get to the glass and concrete **Civic Centre** and its neighbour, the **Nico Theatre Centre**, focus of Cape Town's mainstream entertainment.

At the southern end of the Heerengracht is the railway station, whose precincts embrace a lively fleamarket and the very well organized **Tourism Gateway.**

Cape Town is set for rapid growth; tourism and the conference trade are especially promising, and much of the Foreshore is earmarked for major development.

Above: *Maria, the wife of founder, Jan van Riebeeck.*
Below: *The Heerengracht, Cape Town's broadest and stateliest thoroughfare.*

Adderley Street ✶

The striking feature of the city's busiest street (named after a 19th-century British politician) is the vast **Golden Acre** centre, comprising a cavernous hall and concourses packed with department stores, speciality shops, eateries and cinemas. Its many glittering passageways run maze-like beneath the wider neighbourhood to link (among much

else) the railway station, coach terminal, two parking garages and the skyscraping five-star **Cape Sun Hotel**.

The Golden Acre is thought to be the site of the Dutch settlers' first earth-and-timber fort (the planned site of the Castle was to be about 223m (732ft) further eastward from the fort). A small reservoir, dating back to

1663, was uncovered during building operations of the Golden Acre and a portion remains on display.

Just a few paces further up the bustling Adderley Street are the famed flower-sellers; raucous and good-humoured street vendors who invite bargain and banter and will sell you carnations, irises, roses, gladioli, and proteas – if in season – at surprisingly low prices.

The Dutch Reformed **Groote Kerk**, or 'Great Church', stands further up, on the left. It's a graceful structure, oldest of the country's formal places of worship – it was consecrated only in 1841, but incorporates the steeple and other elements of its 1704 predecessor – and noted for its splendid pulpit, vaulted timber roofing and gravestones that serve as paving slabs. Across the street, more or less opposite, is **Edgars' City Store**, the new flagship of one of the country's most popular clothing chains.

Worth at least an hour or so of sightseeing time is the **Cultural History Museum** at the top of Adderley Street, whose exhibits include thematic displays and a wealth of Oriental and other objets d'art. Rather special are the antique weapons, and the old postal stones that served as 'letter boxes' for the early Dutch trading fleets. The building started life as the slave lodge (and, less formally, as a brothel), and was later converted into the Supreme Court. Let your eyes wander up to the rear pediment carved by Anton Anreith: it bears a caricature of the British Lion and Unicorn, rare humour from an otherwise dour Calvinistic past.

Below: *The cool, stone-flagged interior of the Cultural History Museum, in Adderley Street, originally the slave lodge.*

Opposite, in Wale Street, is **St George's Anglican Cathedral**, where apartheid was often movingly protested. Listen to superb choral music, (note the rose window) and hear the sermons of Archbishop Njongonkulu Ndungane, successor to Nobel Laureate Archbishop Desmond Tutu.

City Centre Stroll **

Perhaps the most pleasant of Cape Town's several piazzas is the graceful and leafy **Greenmarket Square**, where fruit and vegetable growers once marketed their wares. Most of the other open spaces have fallen victim to high-rise development and the need for inner-city parking, but Greenmarket Square has retained its earlier role to add colour and life to the central area. From Monday to Saturday it is crammed to its cobbled limits with umbrella-shaded street-traders' stalls heavy with bric-a-brac, craftwork, creative clothing, leatherware, costume jewellery, fire-sale junk and, occasionally, genuine antiques.

These last are more readily available at nearby **Church Street** and **Burg Street's** paved antique mall.

Girding the small square are some very attractive buildings, notably the Gothic-style **Metropolitan Methodist Church** and the **Old Town House**, built in the 1750s to house the Burgher Senate (city council) and the Burgher Watch, a kind of police force cum fire-fighting squad. On view inside, beneath the star-spangled dome, are fine works of art including the Michaelis Collection, consisting of some 100 masterpieces of old Flemish and Dutch schools.

Running south to north through the city centre is **St George's Mall**, until recently congested with traffic but now brick-paved and reserved for pedestrians with time and a little money to spare. There are upmarket shops and arcades to either side; bistros, kiosks, street stalls and buskers on the paved area.

Long Street, which runs parallel to the Mall, was the liveliest part of 19th-century Cape Town and it still draws bargain-hunters, bibliophiles and serendipity shoppers with its antique and junk outlets, pawnshops

Above: *The stately Houses of Parliament opposite the Company's Garden, on Government Avenue.*

OPEN-AIR SHOPPING

All-purpose street markets, a lively feature of the city scene, are held at
• **Greenmarket Square**
• **Grand Parade**
• **St. George's Mall**
• **Railway station**
• **V & A Waterfront**
(between the Blue Shed and Aquarium.).
Antique Markets
• **Church Street** (daily except Sundays)

MARKET PLACES

Craft markets take place over weekends and public holidays, mostly in the suburbs. Here you'll find a splendid variety of original wares ranging from yellowwood furniture, hand-blown glass, pottery, basketry and inventive jewellery to carpets, tapestries and trendy clothing. Contact Captour for dates and times.

• The **Blue Shed Art and Craft Market**, and the **Red Shed Craft Workshop** – at the V & A Waterfront.

• **Constantia Craft Market**, Kendall Road, Constantia.

• **Groot Constantia Craft Market**, on the Groot Constantia estate.

• **Craft in the Park**, in the Rondebosch Park (corner of Campground and Sandown roads, near the Common).

• **Green Point Stadium Craft Market**, Sea Point.

• **Kirstenbosch Craft Market**, on the corner of Kirstenbosch and Rhodes Drive, opposite the entrance to the botanical gardens.

• **The Meadows Market**, in Meadowridge.

• **Lions Arts and Crafts Market**, Hout Bay Common.

Above: *The filigreed charm of Long Street. Many of the city's facades are being carefully restored.*

Opposite: *The Company's Garden, with cloud-capped Table Mountain in the background. The garden began life, in 1652, as a vegetable patch.*

and second-hand bookshops. Near the corner of Hout and Long Streets is the **Sendinggestig**, the **Missionary Meeting House Museum** and one of the city's more elegant edifices. Inside you'll see a handsome hall, galleries of yellowwood and stinkwood resting on Ionian columns, a splendid pulpit (Chinese Chippendale) and pipe-organ, oak pews and teak balconies, and also displays of early missionary work at the Cape.

The upper end of the thoroughfare boasts some charming late-Victorian buildings (among them the striking-looking **Blue Lodge**), many of which have received facelifts and now stand proud in their filigreed glory. While heading south towards the famous Long Street baths (heated pool, massage, Turkish steam) at the top end of the street, keep an eye open for the **Palm Tree** and **Dorp Street mosques**.

THE GARDENS AREA ★★★

Traffic thunders on all sides, but once you step into the **Company's Garden** – the area of the humble vegetable patch planted by the first Dutch settlers over three centuries ago – you're in an oasis of tranquillity.

This is one of the most beautiful of Africa's urban parks, a spacious (6ha; 15 acres) expanse of manicured lawns, fountains and pools, stately trees, colourful shrubs, wandering pathways and, running along the eastern edge, oak-lined **Government Avenue**; a favourite haunt of Capetonian strollers and of cheeky little grey squirrels. Altogether, the gardens are sanctuary to more than 3000 plant species, most of them exotic. The conservatory at the mountain end contains some fine orchids and palms; close by is an aviary bustling with birds; the tea garden serves rather ordinary fare but its setting is exquisite.

Imposing edifices flank the gardens on three sides. Along the east on Government Avenue are the **Houses of Parliament**, to whose gallery the public has access (guided tours are also conducted during recess periods). The Colonial-Regency style **Tuynhuys**, once a pleasure lodge and now the president's city residence, is next door. Spare a glance for the equestrian statue of General Louis Botha, guerrilla leader during the Anglo-Boer War (1899-1902) and prime minister from 1910 to 1919, that stands on Stal Plein in front (on the Plein Street side) of Tuynhuys.

> **CHEEKY CHUMS**
>
> The lively little **grey squirrels** that delight visitors to the **Company's Garden**, are indigenous to North America. They were introduced to Cape Town in the 1890s by Cape premier **Cecil Rhodes**, and bred so freely that they soon became familiar residents of forests, parks and suburban gardens throughout the region. They live mainly on pine seeds, nuts, acorns and fruits, but they will also rob birds' nests of eggs. They are very tame.

Further up you'll find the **National Art Gallery** – repository of some 6500 works of art, local and European – and another statue, a quite magnificent representation of soldier, statesman and philosopher Jan Smuts. Critics condemned it as a 'grotesque parody' when it was erected in the 1960s – and public outrage forced the commissioning of the much blander version that you'll see at the avenue's northern end in front of the **Cultural History Museum** – but it radiates power and personality.

Then there's the **Great Synagogue**, an impressively domed and twin-towered Baroque building, and its neighbour the **Old Synagogue**, designed during the brief Egyptian Revival architectural period at the Cape and now housing the historical and ceremonial treasures of the **Jewish Museum**. At the top of Government Avenue is **Bertram House**, an elegant Georgian period museum (early 19th-century furniture, Chinese porcelain, English silver).

African culture, the huge variety of about 200 million-year-old fossils

unearthed from the strata of the Great Karoo (including dinocephalians, or 'fearful heads'), and the whales of the southern seas are prominent among the subjects displayed in the **South African Museum**, on the southwestern (Queen Victoria Street) side. Birds, fishes, geology, archaeology and the history of printing also feature. Part of the museum complex is the **Planetarium**, whose projectors reproduce the hemisphere's heavens to illuminate the constellations over a 26,000-year (past, present and future) timespan.

The garden's northern perimeter is graced by the **South African Library**, modelled on Cambridge University's Fitzwilliam Museum and a major reference institution that also contains many Africana and other rare and priceless books.

The Malay Quarter *

Along the slopes of **Signal Hill** to the west of the central area is a dense cluster of dainty little single-storey, flat-roofed houses built during the 18th century for Cape Town's cosmopolitan artisan class. The streets are narrow and steep; many of the buildings are brightly painted; the

minarets of mosques rise above the low skyline, and the call of the muezzin charms the evening air.

This is the Malay Quarter, more correctly known as **Bo-Kaap**, and home to several thousand members of the Cape's Islamic society. Many of the residents are descendants of slaves who, after emancipation in the 1830s, moved into the area to form a very close-knit community,

DISTRICT SIX

East of the city centre is a bare patch of ground that, until 1966, was home to 55,000 mostly **Coloured** people. In that year District Six was declared a 'white' area and officialdom began moving residents to Mitchell's Plain, 30km (19 miles) distant, and other townships on the bleak Cape Flats.

The suburb was demolished – only places of worship escaped the bulldozers – in what was claimed as a slum-clearance programme. District Six had become overcrowded and unsanitary – but it also had vibrancy and a strong sense of community.

The area lay fallow for three decades, an ugly scar on the cityscape and on the conscience of white society. However the land is to be returned to about 45,000 original inhabitants and their descendants. The District Six Beneficiary and Redevelopment Trust, funded by government and private donors, will oversee the development of this important landmark.

bound together by its Indonesian culture and faith. It remains highly integrated. The original Malay tongue is no longer spoken (Afrikaans and English are the home languages) though fragments have survived in the local songs. The community is devoutly **Muslim**.

For the rest, much of the heritage is intact, evident in the religion, in a cuisine that has evolved into a cornucopia of classic Cape dishes, in some of the customs and rituals (including the *Ratiep* sword-dance, led by a *Khalifa*) and, on special occasions, in mode of dress.

A little of this can be seen in the **Bo-Kaap Museum** (71 Wale Street), a 1760s period house and Cape Town's oldest surviving town residence that belonged to the religious leader Abu Bakr Effendi. He hailed from Turkey and, among other things, started an Arabic school in town (he also, oddly enough, wrote one of the first books to be published in Afrikaans). The bedroom is fitted out as a traditional bridal suite; furnishings are typical of an 18th-century Muslim home.

The Bo-Kaap's **Biesmiellah** restaurant serves Malay food (no alcohol allowed). Don't explore the area on your own; tours can be arranged through Captour.

Strand Street

This major thoroughfare once ran along the seafront (before reclamation of the Foreshore) – the name means 'beach' – but now cuts through city-centre, stretching down from Signal Hill to link with the motorways to the northern and southern suburbs.

It's a fairly nondescript street, but it has three points of special interest.

On your left, as you come down the hill, you'll see the dignified facade of the **Lutheran Church**, built in 1771 (and later redesigned) ostensibly as a kind of warehouse – a necessary disguise since, at that time, any form of religious worship other than Dutch Reformed was barely tolerated by officialdom. The entrance, the organ-loft and the splendid pulpit are the work of the sculptor and master-carver Anton Anreith.

Next-door **Martin Melck House**, the original parsonage, is a fine 18th-century Cape Dutch townhouse that has been beautifully restored and now embraces a secluded garden, a charmingly serene tearoom and an elegant restaurant.

The third showpiece is **Koopmans-De Wet House** (35 Strand Street), another classic example of 18th-century Cape domestic architecture. The place was home to Maria Koopmans-De Wet (1838-1906), a leading socialite, connoisseur, patron of the arts,

Afrikaner nationalist and, generally, a formidable political lady who was placed under house arrest for campaigning against the infamous concentration camps of the Anglo-Boer War.

Above: *Koopmans-De Wet House, once home to a leading city socialite and patron of the arts.*
Left: *The old Lutheran Church on Strand Street.*

The interior re-creates the home environment of a rich and fashionable urban family during the last years of Dutch rule. On display are unusual murals, an impressive collection of European and Cape (stinkwood and yellowwood) furniture, beautiful Dutch and German glassware, and some rare porcelain.

THE CASTLE AREA ★★★

The massive, five-sided, stone-walled fort, completed in 1679, was originally designed to guard the fledgling Dutch colony from sea invasion but later served as the military, administrative and social hub of the colony.

The **Castle** has an imposing entrance, embellished with a clock tower, the crest of the United Netherlands, the Dutch East India Company's monogram ('VOC') and the coats of arms of the Company's six chambers in Holland. The tower's bell, cast in 1697, is still rung on occasion. Bisecting the spacious courtyard is a defensive cross-wall known as 'De Kat', which once supported cannon but later became notable for a gracefully balustraded rococo balcony (Klein Kat) that looks down on the onetime governor's residence and the grand reception hall.

Much of the Castle is open to the public. On display in the Governor's residence are period furnishings, objets d'art, ceramics and the celebrated William Fehr Collection (guided tours 10:00, 11:00, 12:00, 14:00, 15:00).

ROYAL VISITOR

Britain's **Queen Elizabeth** made her second trip to Cape Town in March 1995, stepping off the Royal yacht *Britannia* at the Waterfront dockside to be greeted – and introduced to a very changed South Africa – by **President Mandela**. During her two-day stay she addressed a joint sitting of the new and fully democratic parliament, and saw something of the high-density and impoverished township of Khayelitsha. The Queen's previous visit was in 1947 when, as a young Princess Elizabeth, she accompanied the Royal family on the tour of a country still adjusting after the trauma of World War II. She celebrated her 21st birthday at a glittering ball held in Cape Town's stately city hall.

Below: *Much of the Castle, including its historic moat, has been carefully restored.*

The original moat and wooden bridge have been restored; other recent renovations and additions include a military museum, the historic Dolphin Pool, a period house (the Secunde's quarters), two **dungeons** and the Granary that contains artefacts unearthed during restoration work (old Dutch clay pipes, pieces of porcelain, and there is a transverse section of the Castle's original foundation).

Each day of the week at 12:00 you can watch the changing of the guard. The 'ceremony of the keys' takes place at 10:00 on Tuesdays, Thursdays and Saturdays during holidays or on request. A Cultural Studies Centre (CSC) has been established at the Castle and groups of up to 30 are offered on-going lectures and audio-visual material, to understand and learn about the past. To book a session, contact the CSC at the Castle.

Outside the walls, on the western side, is the **Grand Parade**, where colonial troops mustered in their uniformed glory. It is now a 'pay and display' parking area and a not-very-stylish open-air market. It is also where crowds periodically gather in protest or in celebration – here, for instance, Nelson Mandela spoke conciliatory words to a quarter-million throng hours after his release from prison in 1990.

Above: *The entrance to the Castle, completed in 1679 and the country's oldest occupied building.* **Right:** *The turn-of-the-century City Hall, built of ornate granite in the Italian Renaissance style.*

Mandela delivered his address from the balcony of the flanking **City Hall**, a grandly ornate granite and marble edifice designed in the Italian Renaissance style and completed in 1905. Its clock tower modelled on, though just half the size of that of London's Big Ben, houses southern Africa's largest carillon of 39 bells. The main hall, where the Cape Town Philharmonic Orchestra occasionally gives concerts, has a 3165-pipe organ and is venue for the more lavish of civic functions.

TABLE MOUNTAIN ★★★

South Africa's (and one of the world's) best-known physical feature dominates the Peninsula's northern skyline.

The great flat-topped sandstone massif towers 1087m (3566ft) above the city and measures nearly 3km (2 miles) from end to end, and on a sunny day its distinctive shape can be discerned from 200km (124 miles) out to sea. From the summit there are spectacular views of Cape Town, its harbour and Waterfront below, of **Devil's Peak** and **Lion's Head** to either side, of the hazy and majestic Hottentots Holland mountains in the east and Cape Point far to the south.

The heights, though, are often obscured by what's known as the 'tablecloth': dense clouds that billow across its rim to tumble down the northern precipice in a

Left: *Cape Town panorama, with Table Mountain rising 1087m (3566ft) above the city.*

Above, opposite and below: *A montage of Table Mountain. The views from the top are breathtaking.*

> **MOUNTAIN FLORA UNDER THREAT**
>
> Table Mountain's precious flora is under constant assault from several quarters. **Fire** is a perennial hazard: controlled veld-burning stimulates the germination and growth of some species, but often accidental and vandal-triggered conflagrations can devastate the vegetation. **Alien plants** – cluster pine, hakea, Port Jackson willows among them – have rapidly encroached. Some **hikers** have trampled the ground creating erosive gullies. An exotic type of **ant**, brought in from Argentina during the Anglo-Boer War, has interfered with the propagation of many protea species. Many plants are harvested by the **picked-flower** industry.

continuous cascade. The phenomenon is the product of the southeasterly sea-wind ('Cape Doctor'), which can reach speeds of around 100kph (62 mph). It sweeps moisture from False Bay against the massive rampart, causing the droplets to rise, cool and condense into a thick cover. At these times Table Mountain is not accessible to visitors.

The ancient **Hottentots** knew the massif as 'Hoeri Kwaggo' – Mountain of the Sea – but it has had many names. The one that endured was bestowed by the first European to climb to the top: **Antônio de Saldanha**, an adventurous Portuguese admiral who made the ascent in 1503 (he was later to be killed in a skirmish with the westcoast Hottentots).

Saldanha had to beat a way to the top; today five excellent walking paths lead to the summit, and there are many suitable only for experienced climbers.

Those who make their way up the slopes – through the woodlands of the heavily watered backing plateaus – can spot almost half of the 2600-odd plants indigenous to the Cape Peninsula.

The Cableway ***

Most visitors ride up in the shiny new gondolas which replaced the old cable cars when the Table Mountain Aerial Cableway Company upgraded its facilities in 1997.

The new Swiss-manufactured cars, boasting revolving floors and a magnificent 360 deg view over the city and beyond, carry up to 65 individuals at a time. The comfortable six-minute trip may be taken at virtually any time of the year - from 08:00 to 22:00 in summer and autumn (Dec - April), 08:30 - 18:00 in winter and spring (May to Nov) - and the service is only suspended if winds exceed 80 kph - not very common even in windy Cape Town. Fortunately the carrying capacity of the R7-million cars has largely eliminated the seemingly endless queues which plagued the old service and, as a result, prior reservations are no longer taken. The wait is thus short and the rewards breathtaking. Along with the renovation of the cableway system, facilities at both the foot and the top of the mountain have been upgraded, with a smart new restaurant and souvenir outlet at the top and restaurant facilities near the lower station.

To get to the lower terminus, drive up Kloof Nek (the M62 road) or take the Kloof Nek bus, which departs from Adderley Street (outside OK Bazaars) every 30 minutes.

Climbing Up

The more energetic visitor may prefer to make the ascent on foot. Some of the established paths are gentle enough (it is a two-hour uphill walk from the back, or southern slopes, of the mountain), others are more strenuous, and some downright dangerous.

All the routes should be treated with respect. It is easy to get lost, which can be a frightening experience

THE HIMALAYAN TAHR

Hunters long ago slaughtered the region's larger creatures, but Table Mountain's central plateau and slopes, now a protected area, (and a National Monument) still support an impressive array of wildlife. Among the species is an exotic creature called the Himalayan tahr, which is like a cross between a goat and a sheep. The mountain's tahrs are descendants of a pair that escaped from the local zoo in the 1930s, and their numbers have to be strictly controlled in order to preserve the environment.

Above: *A pair of dassies, or rock-rabbits. Here, the species has evolved 'sticky' feet for a better grip on the steep slopes.*
Below: *At the top of Table Mountain, looking south across the expanse of False Bay to Cape Point.*

if the weather turns nasty – as it can do, suddenly and without any warning at all.

Invest in a good map and guidebook (available in city bookshops); choose a route that is well within your physical capability; do not stray from the path; and, if it's your first trip, arrange to make it in the company of someone who knows the terrain. Leave word of your route and estimated time of return with a friend. Wear warm clothing and stout walking shoes.

These are elementary precautions, but a surprising number of **climbers** ignore them – and the mountain regularly takes its toll on human life.

On the Summit

Each year hundreds of thousands of people take the cableway to the summit. At the top there is a **restaurant** and a **souvenir shop** – from where you can send a fax, or mail a letter bearing the Table Mountain postmark. Along the tabletop are some superb observation points. Wall plaques describe the mountain's nature reserve and

the plants that grace the slopes during the different seasons. The walk to **Maclear's Beacon**, the mountain's highest point, takes about 50 minutes.

The best time to make the summertime ascent is probably in the early evening (around 18:00), when you can watch the sun set and the colours change over the sea and land. Then stay on for a pleasant dinner at the restaurant and watch the lights come on in the city and harbour.

The Flanking Peaks *

Also worth exploring are the imposing formations that stand to either side of Table Mountain. To the west you'll see the sugarloaf shape of **Lion's Head** and its attendant ridge, which ends in the 'rump' of **Signal Hill**, the whole vaguely resembling a lion *couchant*.

Above: *One of the steep hiking trails in the mountain's deep ravines.*

You can climb to the top of the 669m (2195ft) **Lion's Head** peak; chain ladders help on the most challenging stretches. There are dramatic views from the crest.

More pleasant and a lot less arduous is the drive up **Signal Hill**, from where the vistas are as rewarding. Each day the noon gun is fired from its emplacement on the hill – a sound which tells Capetonians of their impending lunchbreak, though its real purpose is to remind listeners of those who fought and died in World War I and II. The hill's name derives not from the gun, but from an earlier semaphore station that used to communicate with ships at sea. The area is a favourite spot for picnics.

The drive up will take you past four of the Peninsula's six *kramats* – sacred tombs of Muslim holy men who are believed to extend their protective power over the city.

Devil's Peak, on the left as you look up from the city, is notable for two British blockhouses built on its steep slopes 'to maintain a very fine command of the Bay'. The ascent to the summit, about 1000m (3281ft) above sea level, is only for experienced climbers.

> ### THE EASTERN BUTTRESS
>
> **Devil's Peak**, the high buttress that guards Table Mountain's eastern flank, was once an important part of Cape Town's defence. After British troops invaded and occupied the Peninsula in 1795, their commander General Sir James Craig, built **three blockhouses** on the higher slopes. They were named **King's, Queen's** and the **Duke of York's**. King's later served as a convict station, and is now a historical monument. The peak itself is 1002m (3288ft) high and can be reached only by fit and experienced climbers.

3
The Atlantic Seaboard

For two centuries early Cape Town developed around and relied heavily on its **harbour**, but it wasn't until after the middle of the 19th century that its single jetty was replaced by sturdier installations. In 1860 Prince Alfred tipped the first wagon-load of stone for the new **Alfred basin** (the **Victoria Basin** and the twin signal towers were built in 1883).

Later development reclaimed the present **Foreshore** area from the sea, creating the huge Duncan Dock. Later still came the 366m (1200ft) Sturrock dry-dock, one of the largest in the world; the Robinson graving dock; the Ben Schoeman container terminal; and the enormous precooling stores that handle the Western Cape's bountiful export-fruit harvests.

Table Bay harbour also embraces the **Royal Cape Yacht Club**. The rather exclusive club hosts a number of sleek, handsome, high-tech craft, and their crews, at its clubhouse and marina on Duncan Dock. After a long absence, a growing number of large, glamorous cruise ships are also docking.

But it's the older part of the area, the Victoria and Alfred basins, that draws the interest: they have been transformed into a brilliantly animated tourist playground, that rivals Table Mountain as the region's premier tourist attraction.

The Peninsula's 'Atlantic' coastline runs from Table Bay south for 54km (34 miles) to the edge of the Cape of Good Hope Nature Reserve – a route that unveils land- and seascapes breathtaking in their splendour.

THE OCEAN RACERS

Cape Town harbour features as a major station on some of the world's most prestigious yachting routes, including the bi-annual classic **Cape-to-Rio** race (international entries), the **Whitbread** round-the-world and the **BOC** single-handed round-the-world races. The premier local round-the-buoys event is **Rothmans Week**, which takes place in Table Bay during the month of December.

Opposite: *The broad sweep of Camps Bay.*

THE WATERFRONT ★★★

Not too long ago **Table Bay** and its docklands were very much part of Capetonian daily life, but with land reclamation (the Foreshore) and highway construction the links were severed. Gone was the seafront leisure beach and the small fishing boats (*see* p. 28), to be replaced by oil storage tanks, a wilderness of grimy buildings and barriers, and a raised motorway that stands as a monument to poor planning and taste.

Now sea and city have merged again, reunited by the **Victoria & Alfred Waterfront** scheme, a multi-billion rand venture that has revitalized the docks. It draws its inspiration from successful harbour projects in San Francisco, Sydney and elsewhere, but it is not simply a copy: it is designed to meet local needs; it has its own distinctive personality, and its setting, beneath the moody grandeur of Table Mountain, is both unique and exciting.

Below: *One of the many Cape fur seals that bask at the quayside.*

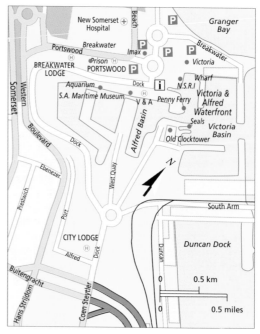

Nor is it just a pleasure-ground. The V & A is still very much a working area; the graving docks, originally built for the tall ships of yesteryear, continue to function; salt-stained fishing craft use the basins; tugs and tour boats move up and down; offices and apartments are being built and new developments are in progress.

For the most part, though, the open quaysides are for tourists and the leisure-bent locals. The scheme is by no means complete, but the more interesting and colourful of the existing structures have already been converted, and a lot of new ones built, to serve as restaurants, hotels, umbrella-shaded bistros, bars, coffee shops, cinemas (including the giant Imax), museums, markets (craft, fish, produce), speciality stores, entertainment centres and the world-class Two Oceans Aquarium (*see* p. 48). Other attractions in progress, or planned, include a small-craft marina, a promenade, public squares, walkways, a steam-railway station and a waterway leading all the way into the city centre.

Sights to See

The Waterfront is for relaxation – for eating, drinking, shopping, and for soaking up the charming atmosphere – rather than for sightseeing. But a fair amount that is of historical interest will emerge as you stroll the precincts.

Left: *BMW Pavilion.*
Right: *The Aquarium.*

THE BIG SCREEN

A must for **Waterfront** visitors is the **BMW Pavilion**, venue for the breathtaking **Imax** cinematic experience, the world's largest film format. The pin-sharp, almost three-dimensional images projected onto the gigantic screen (it is five storeys high), together with powerful multi-speaker digital sound, creates something close to 'virtual reality', bringing you right into the picture. The impact is quite astonishing.

The world-wide Imax enterprise has over 100 productions in its library. Titles shown at the Waterfront's theatre, which opened in 1994 with *The Blue Planet*, a magnificent space film about earth, include *The Rolling Stones at the Max, Everest, Whales, The Grand Canyon* and *African Elephants*.

Take note of the **Time Ball Tower**, once used by pass-ing ships to set their clocks, and the **Old Port Captain's building** (the Waterfront's headquarters). Across the Cut, on the opposite side is the **Old Clock Tower** (which housed the clock mechanism on the topmost floor, and on the bottom floor, the tide-gauge, operated by a float on the water below). Cape fur seals, oblivious of the passing parade, sun themselves around Victoria basin; they're especially fond of the spot near Bertie's Landing.

There is a well-stocked **Wine Centre**, next door to the visitor information office and further along is the small **Mitchell's brewery** that produces superb draught ale.

The **South African Fisheries Museum** is on West Quay Road and offers information on the sea and its resources. The impressive **Union Castle Building** houses the **Telkom Exploratorium** on the first floor, and pro-vides fascinating insights into telecommunications.

Shopping

Principal centre is the huge **Victoria Wharf** shopping mall; a complex of converted warehouses crammed with upmarket outlets ranging from a biltong bar (biltong is dried raw meat, and a prized South African delicacy) through jewellery, clothing and accessories boutiques, to

some of the country's most imaginative craft shops. The Wharf is open till late, seven days a week. Next-door, the **King's Ware-house** houses a cornu-copia of produce and fine-food stores.

Make a point, too, of visiting the **Red Shed** craft workshop (ceramics, jewellery, textiles, basketware, township art, candles) and African Heritage

Opposite: *An outdoor concert draws the crowds.* **Left:** *The imaginatively conceived Waterfront area.* **Bottom:** *Victoria Wharf shopping mall.*

SHOWCASE OF SHIPS

A major waterfront attraction is the **South African Maritime Museum**, whose floating exhibits include the historic *SAS Somerset*, the world's sole surviving boom defense vessel, and the steam tug *Alwyn Vincent*. Both are moored in front of the Victoria & Alfred Hotel. Among much else on view is a shipwright's workshop, a children's 'discovery cove' and intriguing displays relating to shipwrecks, Table Bay harbour (past, present and future), the fishing industry, shipping lines and the romantic era of the Union Castle mailships.

(beadwork, woven goods and much else). There's also the **Waterfront Art and Craft Market**, where you'll find an enormous selection of local handwork.

Other shopping clusters are located at the **Victoria and Alfred Hotel** (the Alfred Mall) and at the **Pierhead**.

Food, Drink and Entertainment

There are restaurants for all preferences and pockets; the menus on offer range from traditional Cape fare and seafood, through Mediterranean, Cajun, Italian, Chinese and Mexican to *haute cuisine*. Several of the eateries are also taverns (**Ferryman's** and **Quay Four** are among the most popular) that occasionally feature live music and entertainment. The **Sports Café** pub and restaurant combines conviviality with sporting interest: television sets beam local and international events while patrons watch, eat, drink and make merry.

International chains are represented by **Planet Hollywood**, and the **Hard Rock Café**, which offer themed family entertainment. A number of coffee bars and bistros cater for those with more sophisticated tastes, while a fast food mall offers a wide variety of 'food to go'. A range of local and imported mineral water is available from a dedicated water bar.

TRIPS AND TOURS BY AIR

For a memorable bird's-eye view of the city and surrounding areas, book a helicopter flip. Companies offer excursions ranging from a ten-minute jaunt around the city bowl and Table Mountain to an hour's flight south along the scenically stunning Atlantic seaboard to Cape Point and back over False Bay. Various tours take you farther afield – to the picturesque Winelands, for instance, where you spend time sightseeing, sampling the vintages and lunching at one of the stately homesteads.
Among aerial tour operators are: Court, Sealink, Civair, Sport Helicopters and Flamingo Flights. Destinations include Hermanus, the Garden Route, Langebaan Lagoon and, in springtime, flower-bedecked Namaqualand.

Below: *Robben Island's Old Residency, once the home of the commissioner.*

PENNY FERRY

A charming way to get across **The Cut** between the V & A Waterfront's **Pierhead** and **East Quay** is to take the Penny Ferry; a venerable little rowboat that makes the voyage in about four minutes. In the early days the trip cost a penny; hence the name. The service is 100 years old 'and still rowing strong', despite the recent installation of a swing bridge across The Cut.

For young people (of all ages) the Waterfront is in fact an Aladdin's Cave of delights. Open-air entertainment, mime-shows and a mime workshop, a gemstone scratch-patch, boat rides, and close encounters with a high-flying trapeze are among the drawcards. Imaginative pirate parties are held aboard the **Victoria Treasure Ship**, where all manner of sea-related exhibits – including gold and silver recovered from shipwrecks – are on view.

Getting Around

For gentle sightseeing, there's the Waterfront historical walk (details from the information centre), round-the-harbour boat trips, and the famous **Penny Ferry**. If you're feeling more adventurous and want a bird's-eye view of the wider scene, take a helicopter flip around the harbour, city bowl or further afield. Sea cruises (to Robben Island, among other destinations), game-fishing excursions and boat charters are also available.

A regular bus service operates between city-centre and the Waterfront. There's ample parking for private cars.

ROBBEN ISLAND *

About 11.5km north (7 miles) out to sea and clearly visible from the shore is oval-shaped Robben Island ('robben' is Dutch for 'seals'), which until recently served as the infamous maximum-security prison, where **Nelson Mandela**, South Africa's first truly democratically elected president, served much of his 27-year sentence.

Today, Robben Island has a new and far more amiable image. Since the early 1990s several concerned groups have been planning its future as a national treasure, including the **Heritage Programme**. Conservationists want to preserve the area as a breeding ground for Caspian and Damara terns, rare jackass penguins and around 30 other bird species, and as a forest reserve. These and its other assets – the wild flowers (arum lilies are everywhere), the rugged coastline, the magnificent vistas across the waters to Cape Town and Table Mountain, and its significance in the liberation struggle – place it high on the list of potential tourist attractions.

The 574ha (1418 acres) island's history goes back a long way. Early Portuguese, Dutch and English mariners on their way to and from the Orient visited its shores for fresh provisions (seals, penguins and birds' eggs), and on two occasions in the early 1600s it was used to confine convicts. Later, the first Dutch colonists collected its seashells (to produce lime), and its 'beautifully veined' slate and dressed stone to construct the Castle and some of infant Cape Town's other buildings.

Over the decades Robben Island also served variously as a giant livestock pen, a place for lunatics and paupers, the chronically sick and otherwise unwanted (their suffering caused a public outcry that eventually put a stop to the abuses), a leper colony – and as a penal colony.

At one stage, the inmates included political prisoners, among them high-born exiles from Holland's Eastern

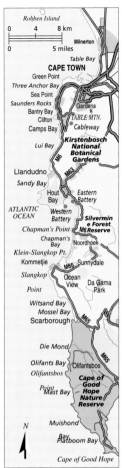

Left: *Bird's-eye view of Robben Island, used over the centuries to confine political prisoners and other 'undesirables'.*

Nelson Mandela, president from 1994 - 1999, was incarcerated for treason on Robben Island.
Born in 1918 into the royal Tembu (Xhosa) house in the Transkei region of the Eastern Cape, Mandela qualified as a lawyer during the 1940s and quickly became prominent in the movement to liberate the country from apartheid, helping found *Umkhonto we Sizwe*, the military wing of the **African National Congress**, in the 1950s. Finally indicted for conspiring to commit nearly 200 acts of sabotage he was convicted at the famed Rivonia trial of 1963 and sentenced to life imprisonment. On his release in 1990 he chose the path of peace, employing his skills and immense moral stature to lead South Africa to freedom and democracy.

possessions such as the Princes of Ternate and Madura. They are commemorated in the island's *kramat*. Another prominent prisoner was the Xhosa prophet Makhanda, who helped lead his people in a 'holy war' against the colonists. He was consigned to Robben Island in 1819, organized a mass escape and was drowned when the boat capsized in a storm.

This living **museum** supports a tiny village of about 1200 inhabitants. Among notable structures are the 1800s lighthouse, which still performs with honour; the **Church of the Good Shepherd**, designed by celebrated turn-of-the-century architect Herbert Baker, and the old **Residency**, once the home of the local commissioners.

Other features date to World War II, when the island figured in Cape Town's sea defences. They include a scatter of buildings, and bunkers to house the 6-inch guns. And, of course, the prison where Nelson Mandela and others spent so many years of their lives.

Only the Robben Island Museum conducts official tours of the island and bookings may be made through the Robben Island Information and Exhibition Centre; tickets may be bought at the Robben Island Museum and the embarkation point at Bertie's Landing, from where the *Makana* departs; entry charges vary; the trip takes about an hour; tours may take up to three hours; tel: 419-1300.

THE RIVIERA

The coastal road that leads southwest from **Table Bay**, traverses an 8km (5 miles) shoreline of rocky indentations, entrancing expanses of white sand and charming little coves around which cluster some of the city's most fashionable residential areas.

Thereafter, the maritime highway – **Victoria Drive** – takes you along the coast through virtually deserted and

scenically stunning landscapes to **Hout Bay** and beyond, to remote **Scarborough**, before turning inland to the **Cape of Good Hope Nature Reserve**.

To drive along this route, at any time of the day but especially at the magical sunset hour, is delight indeed. On your left, for much of the way, are the often cloud-wreathed heights of the **Twelve Apostles**, part of the Table Mountain range. On your right are jagged cliffs that tumble down to rocks and the blue ocean.

Opposite: Sea Point, a cosmopolitan place of smart beachfront apart-ments, a myriad eateries and a stunning promenade. **Above:** *Clifton's beaches in high summer. The water tends to be chilly, but the sands are sheltered from the prevailing wind.*

The Seaside Suburbs *

West of the city is **Green Point**, noted for its pleasant Common and golf course (the Metropolitan). The Green Point Lighthouse is the oldest in the country: its giant oil lantern first shone in 1824, later to be replaced by an 850,000-candlepower lamp that can be seen 23km (14 miles) out to sea. The local hospital, New Somerset (actually over 100 years old) houses the Cape Medical museum, worth a visit for its fascinating relics of modern medicine's pioneering days. Of special interest is the re-created Victorian dentist's surgery. Also note the photograph of the somewhat effeminate Dr James Barry, who performed the country's first Caesarean section and went on to become inspector-general of Britain's army hospitals. On his death, so the story goes, it was revealed that Barry was a woman, though the story was never conclusively substantiated.

Next-door **Sea Point** is a busy, bustling, cosmopolitan area dense with luxurious apartment and time-share blocks, hotels, restaurants, discos, delis and nightspots. The Main Road is a glitzy, noisy, fun thoroughfare, though the tinsel is a bit tarnished in

places (it has lost much of its custom to the harbour Waterfront). The long, (3km; 2 miles) lawn- and palm-graced promenade is much favoured by Capetonian strollers. At the end of Beach Road is the Sea Point Pavilion. Main features are the large seawater swimming pool, a restaurant and fast-food and icecream outlets.

From Sea Point you drive through **Bantry Bay** to **Clifton**, famed for its four inviting beaches, each divided from its neighbour by a jumble of granite boulders and sheltered from the southeaster wind. Third Beach is popular among the trendy young while Fourth Beach is usually packed with families. Note that parking is a problem; only Fourth has vehicular access. There aren't many visitor facilities – the suburb has managed to resist commercial inroads, retaining its quiet dignity at the expense of tourism infrastructure.

The hillside slopes support the houses of the rich (and occasionally famous); beyond, towering high above suburb and sea, are the backing massifs: **Lion's Head** and the first of the Apostles that form the western coastal rampart. They are infinitely changeable in their mood, and breathtaking in their grandeur. Hugging the sheer cliffside below the road are massed banks of luxury apartments and houses.

Camps Bay, further along, also boasts a fine expanse of sand, but has more amenities (tidal pool, shops, theatre, restaurants, and an excellent hotel called The Bay), though both centres remain affluent residential areas rather than playgrounds.

A digression up Kloof Road will lead you to the Round House, built in the last century as a shooting lodge which has since become a restaurant and to The Glen, a pleasant picnic spot with lovely views.

HOUT BAY ★★★

After a twisting and visually spectacular 15km (9 miles) drive along the coast road you'll see, nestled among the rocks far below on your right, the picture-postcard village of **Llandudno**. It rests in a precipitous valley beneath a peak known as Little Lion's Head, and boasts a lovely, secluded beach (the flanking **Sunset Rocks** invite quiet contemplation at twilight) and its own shipwreck.

Walk for about 20 minutes down the shoreline and you'll get to **Sandy Bay**, prime venue for those in search of an all-over tan. Much larger than Llandudno but equally attractive is adjacent **Hout Bay**, a fishing harbour and rapidly growing residential town girded by magnificent mountain slopes. 'Hout' is the Afrikaans word for 'wood': the name derived from the area's value as a source of timber in the early colonial days. But the hillsides are still reassuringly tree-mantled.

Hout Bay's picturesque, small harbour is the headquarters of the Peninsula's crayfish (rock lobster) fleet; other catches include tasty snoek, which is sold on the quay in June and July. The annual **Snoek Festival** occupies a lively weekend during this period; busy throughout the year is

Opposite above: *Luxurious residences hug Clifton's seafront.*
Opposite below: *The charming seaside village of Llandudno. Beyond is risqué Sandy Bay.*
Below: *Viewing peaceful Hout Bay from Chapman's Peak Drive. The imposing massif at the left is known as The Sentinel.*

SANDY BAY

Until recently this was South Africa's only nude beach although not officially recognized as such. It tends to be a bit crowded, but there's more to the place than nubile nudity: the steeply rising hinterland is covered by the Cape's unique *fynbos* vegetation, and there's pleasant seclusion to be found among the beachfront boulders.

HOUT BAY WALKS

The Hout Bay area is splendid hiking and rambling country. Especially rewarding is the 12km (7 miles) scramble over the lower slopes of the towering **Sentinel** and **Karbonkelberg** peaks to Llandudno. Take the three-hour stroll to **Myburgh's Waterfall**, on the wooded southern flanks of the **Table Mountain** range. Bright red disas decorate the ravine and the fringes of the waterfall in summertime. For scenic splendour, though, nothing can rival the climb up **Chapman's Peak**: from the summit you look down on the town and its harbour; in the distance is the great sweep of Noordhoek beach and, across the Peninsula, the shores of False Bay. Mike Lundy's *Twenty Walks around Hout Bay* is an invaluable guide to the various routes.

Mariner's Wharf, a complex modelled on its namesake in San Francisco and embracing seafood bistro, restaurant, fresh fish and live lobster market (also on sale are closed oysters; any pearls you find are yours to keep), nautical gift and curio shops. Across the road is **Dirty Dick's** and **The Big Blue,** a lively tavern complex with fine views over the harbour. Battered working boats and squeaky-clean leisure craft rub shoulders along the moorings.

Several boat companies takes sightseers on sunset 'champagne' **cruises** to Cape Town's Waterfront, 20km (12 miles) distant, and on shorter trips to nearby **Duiker Island**, where in summertime a myriad seabirds – most of them fairly rare Bank cormorants – and more than 4000 Cape fur seals bask on the rocky shores. Seals are common inhabitants of the Peninsula and west coast, remarkably comfortable in the presence of people and so numerous that commercial fishermen claim they make serious inroads into marine resources. The culling of seals – both to control their numbers and for their meat, blubber and pelts – has provoked fierce controversy.

Charter companies advertise deep-sea **game-fishing** (contact Captour for details) and other attractions include the **Hout Bay Museum** (information on guided walks available) and the **World of Birds**.

Below: *A trip to Duiker Island seal sanctuary.*

CHAPMAN'S PEAK AND BEYOND **

Southward still, the coast road cuts through the multi-coloured strata of towering cliffs.

Chapman's Peak Drive is one of the region's finest scenic routes. Winding precariously along the mountain for 10 km (6 miles) from Hout Bay to Noordhoek, the heart-stopping highway twists its way 600m (1970 ft) to the highest point to reveal views of memorable splendour, including the view northwards towards **Hout Bay** with its distinctive **Sentinel buttress** and the distant green hills of **Constantia**.

Left: Chapman's Peak Drive, among the world's most spectacular routes.
Below: Long Beach.

As Chapman's Peak Drive ends, you come into the lagoon-laced **Noordhoek** flatlands, fringed by **Long Beach**.

Noordhoek is still rural – charmingly so – and the haunt of an unusual number of artists and craftspersons. The Horse Trail Safaris and Dunes stables organize beach rides; contact Captour for details.

From here you can either head across the waist of the Peninsula to the **False Bay** town of **Fish Hoek** or take the M65 south to **Kommetjie**, a delightful little seaside centre that offers good angling, surfing, bird-watching and (rather chilly) bathing. After Kommetjie is **Scarborough**; a cluster of holiday houses set in a wilderness of heath.

BIGGEST BIRD PARK

Don't miss **Hout Bay's World of Birds**, the largest bird park in Africa – and imaginatively conceived. Its 100 or so spacious walk-through aviaries are landscaped to provide habitats natural to about 3000 residents, which represent 450 different species. Visitors wander at will through the enclosures while the birds carry on with their busy routines – feeding, building nests, bathing, socializing – oblivious of the human presence. In and around the willow-shaded ponds are freer birds, including cormorants, herons, egrets and swans. There are also endearing monkeys and meercats.

NOORDHOEK ART ROUTE

Artists and craftspersons of Noordhoek welcome visitors to their studios, to view their wares and watch them at work. A selection of their art is also on display and for sale at Under the Rainbow Gallery, among the stately milkwood trees of the **Chapman's Bay Trading Centre**, on Beach Road. The centre also includes The Red Herring Restaurant, the Garden Fair Nursery, Wildside Café, and Clay Connections which sells pottery. Brochure available from Captour.

4
The Eastern Seaboard

The Peninsula's eastern coastline, from **Cape Point** to **Cape Hangklip**, is lapped by the warm and often wind-tossed waters of **False Bay,** one of coastal South Africa's foremost holiday playgrounds.

False Bay's rather odd name derives from the less benevolent side of its nature. Many an early seafarer mistook the Point for Hangklip and thought they were in Table Bay – a serious navigational error – and over the centuries ships were regularly driven ashore by the perverse winds and currents. The sea here still, occasionally, takes its toll of traffic, but for the most part the shores are kindly, a mecca for the bather and boating enthusiast, the fisherman and the underwater explorer.

THE CAPE OF GOOD HOPE NATURE RESERVE

Almost 8000ha (19,770 acres) of the Peninsula's southern section is occupied by the Cape of Good Hope Nature Reserve, a rather bleak but plant-rich expanse of *fynbos* (heather) **vegetation** that, come springtime, is magically transformed by multicoloured swathes of wild flowers.

The reserve has few trees – just a scatter of wind-bent milkwoods manage to withstand the fierce southeasterly winds – but more than 1200 flowering species have been identified within its bounds, and more, as yet unlogged, await the inquisitive botanist. It also sustains wildlife: **Cape mountain zebra**, **Cape fox, caracal** and a variety of **antelope**, including the once-threatened but now flourishing **bontebok**. The area is home, too, to about five troops of **chacma baboons**.

BEWARE THE BABOONS

The chacma baboons of the **Cape of Good Hope Nature Reserve** are thought to be the only primates in the world (apart from fish-eating man) that live, largely, off the fruits of the sea, which they garner from the rockpools and beaches at low tide. The baboons are partial to human handouts but in your own interest, and in theirs, keep your vehicle locked and *do not feed them.*

Opposite: *Villages gird the shores of False Bay.*

Above: *Looking down from Cape Point.* **Opposite:** *The Vasco da Gama monument.*

EXPLORING ON FOOT

Visitors are free to walk where they wish in the Cape of Good Hope Nature Reserve, though seven routes have been charted and sign-posted. These range from the one-hour Kanonkop Trail on the eastern side to the four-hour (one-way) Good Hope Coastal Walk that takes you from Cape Point along the western shoreline from near Cape Point to the wreck-site of the good ship *Phyllisia*. A map of the trail network is available at the reserve's entrance, and the informa-tion centre will bring you up to date on the on-going pro-gramme of walks and trails. About 20km (12 miles) of tar and gravel roads are also open to mountain bikers; for information, contact Day-trippers, tel: (021)531-3274.

Over 160 different kinds of **avifauna** have been recorded within the reserve, including the tiny **sunbird**, the **black eagle** and such ocean-going species as **albatross**, **cormorant** and the **ostrich**.

The terrain, broken by a ridge of hills running down the False Bay side, is cut through by a network of roads and trail-paths that lead to picnic and barbecue sites, beaches, coves and viewing points.

Despite some concern for the ecology of the region, facilities for the almost half a million annual visitors have recently been upgraded to include the new Two Oceans Restaurant, fast becoming one of the peninsula's favourite dining experiences, and a new funicular to ferry visitors to the exceptional viewing spots. Other amenities include an information centre, a souvenir shop, a small slipway, tidal pools and superb scuba-diving and snorkelling spots. On calm days, underwater visibility is good, and the marine life both colourful and fascinating.

Cape Point ★★★

The reserve's chief drawcard is unquestionably the massive and spectacular headland at the tip of the Peninsula. Cape Point's cliffs fall sheer for about 300m (985ft) to the ocean, in whose often turbulent waters you can glimpse shoals of **tuna** and **snoek**, sporting **dolphins**

and **seals** and, occasionally, the massive bulk of a **southern right whale**. **Albatross**, **petrel**, **gannet** and **gull** wheel and cry in the air around the promontory.

Breathtaking vistas unfold from the base of the old (1857) lighthouse at the top: from here your eye takes in the far ocean horizons and the sweep of **False Bay** to **Danger Point**, 80km (50 miles) to the east.

Cape Point has its place in seafaring myth. It is off this headland that the *Flying Dutchman*, a phantom sailing ship with tattered sails and storm-swept decks, has periodically been sighted. Legend has it that a 17th-century Dutch captain, Hendrik van der Decken, his craft crippled by the southern gales, vowed to round the 'Cape of Storms' even if it took him until the Day of Judgement to achieve.

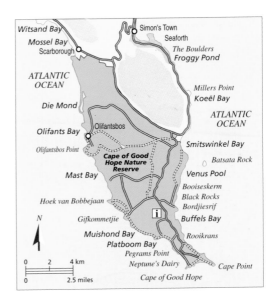

Best-known of the many sightings was that recorded in 1880 by a Royal Navy officer, a young midshipman who, in 1907, became Britain's King George V.

FALSE BAY

From the Cape of Good Hope Nature Reserve northwards, the bay is fringed by a 30km (19 miles), almost continuous, stretch of beach. A number of old, established and attractive seaside centres are also linked together, and to Cape Town, by an excellent road and frequent rail services. Take the slow train along the scenic coastline from Muizenberg to Simon's Town – one of the most stunning train trips in the world – and stop for lunch at the Brass Bell restaurant, perched on the water's edge at Kalk Bay.

Simon's Town ★★★

This substantial and handsome bayside centre is steeped in naval history: it was founded by and named after the energetic Cape governor, Simon van der Stel, in 1687. The harbour provided a valuable anchorage during the Dutch colonial era and, after the British formally took over in 1814, served as the Royal Navy's main South Atlantic base.

It's still very much a naval town but not exclusively so. Commercial and leisure craft crowd the harbour (the **False Bay Yacht Club** is headquartered here), souvenir and craft shops abound. The local beaches are very enticing: **Seaforth, Foxy** beach and their surrounds offer secluded stretches of sand and inlets; **Boulders** beach is famous for its colony of endangered and endearing jackass penguins.

Below: *Simon's Town's main street, known as the Historical Mile.*

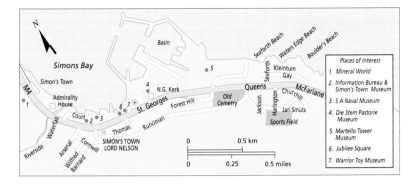

History, though, is the focus. More than 21 of the buildings that line the main street started life over 150 years ago (which is old for South Africa); much of the past has been preserved in the various museums; a Saturday morning guided walk through Simon's Town's **Historical Mile** leaves from the railway station to finish up at East Dock Yard (booking advisable).

The splendid **Old Residency** (now the Simon's Town Museum and the tourist information office) was built in 1777 as the governor's out-of-town hideaway or week-end retreat, later doing successive duty as slave quarters, prison and hospital and now a showcase of naval memorabilia – including mementos of Lord Nelson and a mock-up of a World War II pub – and various cultural collections.

One of the more appealing of the Residency's displays relates to **Just Nuisance**, the beloved Great Dane dog who befriended British sailors during World War II. During his lifetime he was formally ranked as an Able Seaman; on his death he was buried, with full military honours, on a hill overlooking town. A bronze statue of the dog stands in **Jubilee Square**.

Ships, sailors and the sea are also featured, in somewhat greater depth, in the **South African Naval Museum** on West Dockyard. Here there are dioramas of the town and its docks, insights into the realm of coastal defence and much else.

ANTHEMS AND EMBLEMS

Die Stem Pastorie in Simon's Town, once the Dutch Reformed Church's local parsonage, houses an intriguing collection of exhibits devoted to South Africa's various emblems. It was here, in 1919, that the Reverend M.L. de Villiers composed the words for *Die Stem van Suid Afrika*, which eventually became the national anthem – a distinction it now shares with the moving hymn *Nkosi Sikel' iAfrika*. De Villiers' piano is on view, as are displays relating to the national flower (the king protea), bird (the blue crane), tree (the yellowwood) and coat-of-arms, which is based on images descriptive of the country's four former provinces. The complicated and at times controversial story of the national flag is also featured.

Not too long ago on the geo-physical calendar the 'waist' of the Peninsula – the low-lying plain running across its width between Fish Hoek and Noordhoek – lay beneath the sea. Go back about 30,000 years, to a time before the last great Ice Age, and you would find that the ocean level was 20m (70ft) above what it is today, and islands in place of unbroken terrain. During the next 20,000 icy years the level dropped a dra-matic 120m (nearly 400ft) and then, as the climate warmed, rose again – but not to its original height. The Peninsula thus assumed its present character little more than 10,000 years ago.

Of quite different appeal are the **Warrior Toy Museum** in St George's Street, where you'll find an intriguing display of dolls, lead soldiers, miniature cars and trains. Finally, there's **Die Stem Pastorie**, devoted to South Africa's national emblems.

Just outside Simon's Town, up Dido Valley Road, you'll find **Topstones Mineral World**, reputed to be the world's biggest gemstone tumbling factory. Here you can watch huge quantities of rough stone converted into polished sparklers, which are then drilled and fashioned into jewellery and souvenirs. Visitors, especially chil-dren, are also invited to visit the cave and fossick in the scratch patch; a large heap of fragments. What you select you can keep, for a small fee.

Fish Hoek **

A solidly respectable seaside town (until recently it was the only 'dry' municipality in South Africa: no alcohol could be sold within its bounds) noted chiefly for its fine

family beach and the warm summertime off-shore waters bright with yachts, sailboards and catamarans. The gentle **Jager Walk**, along the shoreline rocks, fills a pleasant hour. The rock-pools are very popular with young children. The exhibits of the **False Bay Fire Museum** – fire equip-ment old and new, local and imported – can be viewed by appointment. High above the valley that forms the 'waist' of the

Above: *The beach at Fish Hoek, one of False Bay's larger towns. Jager Walk is a pleasant seafront stroll.*

Peninsula, is the celebrated **Peers Cave**, an important archaeological site and, some 15,000 years ago, home to Fish Hoek Man. The walls are decorated with prehistoric paintings and there are lovely views from the summit.

Left: The pretty little village and harbour of Kalk Bay is the venue for a busy quayside fish market. The hills behind are cut through by labyrinthine caves.

FRESH FISH ON SALE

At around noon each day **Kalk Bay's** little fishing boats return to harbour laden with the fruits of the sea, which are then auctioned off in lively and good-humoured fashion from the quayside. The prices are attractively low, and you can have your fish cleaned on the spot, fresh and ready to take home for the traditional South African '*braai*' (barbecue).

Kalk Bay ★★

An enchanting little harbour and resort village further up the coast. 'Kalk' is the Afrikaans word for 'lime', and the bay was so named because all the shells collected along the coast were burnt there to provide whitewash and mortar for colonial buildings. Today the main commercial activity is fishing; catches are sold on the quayside; the place is especially lively during June and July, when the snoek are running. Along the Main Road and alleys in the village are antique, pottery and junk shops, art galleries and restaurants.

Just behind the coastline, between the village and Muizenberg, are the Kalk Bay mountains, a modest but scenically striking range of hills cut through by a labyrinth of underground chambers. Many have oddball names (Mirth Parlour, Dolly's Doorway, Light and Gloom, Creepy Corridor), and they're worth exploring, though it's suggested you do so with someone who knows their way around. The wild and rocky area is also a magnet for hikers, ramblers, bird-spotters and lovers of nature.

The Muizenberg Area ★

A century ago Capetonian gentlefolk and the millionaire holidaymakers from the goldfields of the north flocked to what was then one of the southern hemisphere's pre-

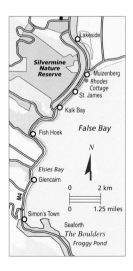

Above: *Muizenberg is famed for its long, broad white sands and its rather old-fashioned charm. The coast is very popular with surfers and fishermen.*

SEASIDE STROLL

Attractive features of **St James** are its gaily painted Victorian-type wooden bathing huts, its safe tidal pool, sheltered beach and rockpools bright with marine life. There is a very pleasant 3km (2 miles) walkway leading along the shoreline to **Muizenberg**. Points of interest en route (along Main Road and reached via a subway); include Rhodes Cottage and the Rust en Vrede mansion, designed by the celebrated architect Sir Herbert Baker in Cape Dutch Revival style. Die Posthuys, which is a white-washed cottage, and Muizenberg railway station, are proclaimed national monuments.

---

mier seaside resorts. **Cecil Rhodes**, Cape premier, financial wizard and megalomaniac empire-builder, died in 1902 in his small, plain, thatch-roofed, stone-walled holiday cottage just off the Main Road between **St James** (also worth a visit for its attractive bathing huts, tidal pool and beach) and Muizenberg.

The house has been preserved as a museum; photographs and personal memorabilia recall the life and times of one of colonial South Africa's most controversial figures. Closer to **Muizenberg** is **The Fort**, an impressive Italianesque building that houses the old masters of the **Natale Labia Museum**; also on view are examples of the modern English painting school and some fine furniture. Further along Main Road is the **South African Police Museum** and **Die Posthuys**. The latter dates back to 1673 (this makes it the country's oldest European house) and served then as a signal house and small fort.

The town's genteel past is reflected in the Victorian villas, Edwardian boarding houses, renovated cottages and the imposing ediface on the railway station designed by Sir Herbert Baker. The candy-striped pavilion offers swimming, miniature-train rides, boat trips, a waterslide and playground.

Another of Rhodes's friends, Rudyard Kipling, wrote evocatively of the 'white sands of Muizenberg, spun before the gale' and indeed the beach is special: a broad, long, gently sloping, expanse of pale sand rhythmically pounded by long lines of breakers. Surfers love the place; so do board-sailors, yachtsmen, water-skiers and dog-walkers. Colourful bathing huts line the beach. There are plans to redevelop much of the beachfront and recapture Muizenberg's former glory.

POSTAL PIONEER

Muizenberg's post office was the first in Africa to receive airmail: on 27 December 1911 South African pilot **Evelyn Driver**, a superb 'instinctive navigator' who had earlier helped pioneer Britain's Royal Mail Aerial Service, delivered 729 specially designed postcards from the Cape Town suburb of Kenilworth. The 12.8km (8 miles) flight, in a Bleriot monoplane, lasted seven and a half minutes.

Further down the coast you'll find some of the biggest and best of beaches – specifically, **Sunrise** and **Mnandi** – but this section of the seaboard is quite undeveloped. It does, though, serve the high-density areas of the Cape Flats, and recreational amenities are improving.

Above: The placid waters of the Silvermine Nature Reserve's upland reservoir. The area offers attractive walking trails.

The noted **Silvermine Nature Reserve** extends inland from the Muizenberg area. On the northern side of town is a delightful stretch of water called **Sandvlei**, favoured haunt of canoeists and watersportsmen. The eye-catching waterfront suburb of **Marina da Gama** flanks the lake's eastern shore.

Also north of Sunrise beach, in the low-lying, sandy terrain between suburb and coastal dune, is a scatter of shallow lakes cherished for their bird life. Well worth a visit is the **Rondevlei Nature Reserve** (Perth Road, Grassy Park), home to 225 different species, most of them waterfowl. Notables include the Caspian terns, the martial eagle and the African fish eagle. A few hippos hide away among the reeds. Hides, look-out towers equipped with telescopes, a waterfront walkway and a very interesting museum feature among the facilities.

ANNUAL EVENTS (CAPE TOWN AND PENINSULA)	
January: The Minstrel (Coon) Carnival, at New Year. J & B Metropolitan Handicap, the Cape's top horse race (3rd Saturday). Cape-to-Rio yacht race (alternate years). Shakespeare season at the Maynardville Open-air Theatre. Opening of Parliament. **March:** University of Cape Town Rag Week. Community Chest Carnival (at Maynardville). Cape Argus-Pick 'n Pay Cycle Tour. Nederburg wine auction at Paarl.	**April:** Two Oceans Marathon (Easter Sunday). Easter Regatta at Simon's Town. **May:** Whale-watching season begins. **July/August:** The Snoek Derby (in Hout Bay). **September:** Spring Wild Flower Show, Kirstenbosch. Whale-watching at its peak. Waterfront Wine Festival. **October:** Spring Regatta (Table Bay). Boland Bank Cycle Race. **December:** Rothmans Sailing Week (Table Bay).

5
Central Peninsula

The Peninsula's inland reaches – those that lie to the west of the suburban line of rail – are hilly and well treed. The woodlands are at their densest and most enchanting on the **Constantiaberg** and in the valleys that sweep down from the southern part of Table Mountain.

The main inland motorway (the M3, which starts off as De Waal Drive and then undergoes several name changes: Rhodes Drive, Paradise, Edinburgh and finally called the Simon van der Stel highway) runs through the southern suburbs. These are heavily populated but, still, the route is for the most part a scenic delight.

GROOTE SCHUUR

The original Groote Schuur Estate (renamed Genadendal by Nelson Mandela), bequeathed to the nation by 19th-century politician and tycoon Cecil Rhodes, covers the mountain slopes beneath Devil's Peak and extends over parts of the Observatory, Mowbray, Rosebank and Rondebosch residential areas. Its most noteworthy component is perhaps the **Groote Schuur** ('Great Barn') homestead itself, which began life in the mid-1600s as Van Riebeeck's granary and, after a chequered· career, was redesigned in imposing, though essentially simple, style by the turn-of-the-century architect Herbert Baker. It is for occupation by the president, if he so chooses.

More accessible, and more visible, is the **University of Cape Town**, the country's oldest and arguably most attractive. The ivy-covered buildings of its upper campus hug the hillside overlooking the highway; its medical

MEDICAL BREAKTHROUGH

Groote Schuur Hospital, is the venue of the world's first human heart transplant. In 1967 Prof. **Christiaan Barnard** and his cardiac team implanted the heart of a 25-year-old accident victim into a middle-aged patient, **Louis Washkansky**, who, battling the effects of anti-rejection drugs, lived for just 18 more days before succumbing to pneumonia. Nevertheless the operation was considered a success.

Opposite: *Superb vistas from Rhodes Memorial.*

Right: *Rhodes Memorial is a monument to Rhodes, who bequeathed his land to the people of South Africa.*

school is housed in nearby Groote Schuur Hospital where, in 1967, Chris Barnard and his cardiac team performed the world's first human heart transplant operation.

For tea, scones and a quiet, relaxing hour in the loveliest of surrounds, take the **Rhodes Memorial** off-ramp just beyond the university. This leads around and back up the mountainside to the unashamedly Imperialistic 'temple' that commemorates a man who, whatever his faults, strode like a Colossus across the Victorian colonial scene. The grand neo-Classical structure, also the work of Herbert Baker, incorporates a powerful piece of statuary entitled Physical Energy by F.G. Watts, together with the four pairs of lion-sphinxes and a bust of Rhodes by J.W. Swan, beneath which is inscribed Kipling's moving tribute to 'the immense and brooding spirit'.

Map legend:

Cableway
Rosebank
Bridgetown
Mostert's Mill
Hazendal
Rhodes Memorial
N
TABLE MTN.
Rondebosch
Athlone
Newlands
Boshof Gates
M4
Bishops Court
Claremont
Crawford
Kirstenbosch Botanical Gardens
Kenilworth
Lansdowne
Race Course
M63
M3
Constantia
Wynberg
Alphen
M1
Ottery
Tokai Plantation
Plumstead
Groot Constantia
M4
M5
Klein Constantia
M42
M3
Diepriver
Lotus River
Buitenverwachting
Heathfield
Grassy Park
Constantia Uitsig
Rondevlei Nature Reserve
Tokai Manor House
Retreat
0   2 km
Steenberg
Tokai
Pollsmoor Prison
0   1.25 miles

Observatory and Rosebank *

The first of these suburbs took its name from the Royal (now the South African National) Observatory, established in 1821 in what was then a wilderness infested by snakes, hippos and leopards.

Further along, on Rosebank's Cecil Road, is the **Irma Stern Museum**, which features the works of one of the country's most prolific and controversial artists. Stern gave the first of her many one-woman shows in Berlin in 1919 but on her return to South Africa her rich, sensual canvases were dismissed as 'revolutionary' (and even immoral), and it wasn't until the 1930s that she began to gain local acceptance. She died in 1966. On display in her Rosebank home, The Firs, are some 200 of her paintings, together with sculptures and her fine collection of antiques, objets d'art and African artifacts brought back from the Congo (Zaire).

Among other elements of the original estate in Main Road, Rondebosch, are the **Baxter Theatre Complex** (*see* p. 22) and **Mostert's Mill**, a traditional Dutch windmill (it is one of only two in the Cape) on De Waal Drive. The mill, which dates to 1796, has been carefully restored and is open to the public. Rondebosh is a university suburb, with many students living in 'digs' in the area.

Below: *Historic Mostert's Mill offers visitors some insight into days of old.*

(*see* p. 22)

EXPLORING THE SOUTHERN SKIES

The South African National Observatory, just off Liesbeeck Parkway in the suburb of Observatory, is the national headquarters of a network of sky-probing installations that includes the advanced complex at **Sutherland**, in the clean-aired Great Karoo far to the north. Of special interest to local astronomers have been the so-called variable stars, whose nature indicates the distance of the Magellanic Clouds. The calculation of this, in turn, helps determine the size (and therefore the age) of the universe itself. The Cape Town arm of the National Observatory sets South African standard time, and also sends the electrical impulse that fires the familiar noonday gun on Signal Hill. Tours are conducted on the second Saturday of each month, by appointment.

Newlands **

This sprawling, fashionable suburb, about 6km (4 miles) from city centre, is noted for its densely treed avenues, its international **cricket** and **rugby** grounds, and its unusually high rainfall – the product of wind patterns and the high mountain backdrop.

For rugby enthusiasts, especially, Newlands is something of a mecca. The recently expanded

THE HOME OF RUGBY

Norwich Park, Newlands is the historic and handsome venue for provincial and international matches and host for the opening ceremony of the 1995 **Rugby World Cup**, which the national Springbok side went on to win. A frequent suburban train service ferries spectators directly to the 50,000-capacity arena. The country's major provincial competition is the **Currie Cup**, contested by the regional unions. Of these, the top three have in the past gone on to take part in the southern hemisphere's 'Super 12' tournament comprising teams from South Africa, New Zealand, Australia and the Pacific islands (Tonga, Western Samoa, Fiji).

THE GENTLER GAME

Newlands cricket ground at Norwich Oval, with its stately oak and plain trees and Table Mountain backdrop, is among the world's most attractive pitches. Here, on lazy summer days, you can watch four-day provincial **Castle Cup** matches and occasional five-day **Tests** against a touring side. Cricket of a different, more lively kind is on view during the one-day internationals and the day-night provincial series (known informally as the 'pyjama game' for the bright team-colours worn by the players).
Match details are published in local newspapers.

stadium hosted the opening match of the 1995 World Cup, among the latest of a long sequence of significant contests stretching back to 1891, when W.E. Maclagen led the first British team onto a South African field (the tourists conceded just one try in a series of 19 games played countrywide). In the decades that followed, South Africa reached and maintained a pre-eminent position in international rugby until its enforced isolation during the wilderness years of apartheid. Much of the story is told by the **South African Rugby Museum**, largest of its kind in the world.

On the Liesbeeck River close to the stadium is the **Josephine Mill**, built in 1840, named in honour of the Crown Princess of Sweden, who later became queen, and now Cape Town's only surviving watermill. There are guided tours and daily milling demonstrations (wholewheat flour is produced in much the same way as it was 150 years ago, ground flour and biscuits for sale), a restaurant and pleasant tea-garden.

Sunday concerts are held outdoors at the mill in summer (November to February) starting at 17:30.

Off the M3 highway, to your right as you drive away from the city (after the University of Cape Town), you'll see the tall trees of **Newlands forest**, a delightful place for picnics and barbecues and much favoured by brisk walkers, hikers and joggers.

Claremont and Wynberg *

Claremont, one of the country's fastest-growing commercial centres, is especially enticing: its sophisticated **Cavendish Square** and **Link** complexes offer a kaleidoscope of all-purpose stores, speciality outlets, excellent restaurants, snack bars, bistros, cinemas and art galleries.

Opposite: *The sylvan tranquility of Newlands forest.*
Left: *Action, atmosphere... cricket fever reaches its peak at the Newlands grounds.*

LADY ANNE'S LEGACY

Lady Anne Barnard was one of London's best hostesses – she numbered Dr Samuel Johnson, William Pitt and the Prince of Wales among her friends – before her arrival in 1797, soon after the first British Occupation (her husband, Andrew, had been appointed colonial secretary at the Cape). Her charm and natural diplomacy did much to win the locals over to the new regime, but her main gifts to posterity were the journal she kept, and the many letters she wrote describing the people of and life in the new colony. Both the journal and the letters were embellished with her skilful sketches. Her beautiful Newlands home, built in 1799, is now the famous Vineyard Hotel.

The Arderne Gardens in Main Road, Claremont, are also worth a visit – for their magnificent exotic trees (cedars, cypresses, Norfolk pines among others) and for the fragile delicacy of their Japanese section.

Wynberg is known for its **Village**, a charming cluster of pre-1850 Chelsea style cottages and antique shops. The nearby **Maynardville Open-air Theatre** is a well-patronized venue for Shakespearean productions during January and February, as well as the annual **Community Chest Carnival,** a fund-raising event that features the food and music of the Cape's many cultures.

THE CONSTANTIA AREA

Constantia is not so much a suburb as a semi-rural and rather lovely swathe of valley, hill, wooded parkland and smart homes hidden discreetly among the trees. It is a very sought-after residential area. The valley also sustained South Africa's first vineyards (*see* p. 13), and its historic estates enjoy an honourable place in the world of wine.

Kirstenbosch ★★★

The gardens that sprawl over some 530ha (1310 acres) of Table Mountain's well-watered southern slopes were founded in 1913 to preserve and propagate South Africa's rich floral heritage, and are today recognized as one of the world's most respected botanical enterprises.

The grounds embrace about half the country's 18,000 species of flowering plant, among them the proteas and ericas of the Cape's unique *fynbos* vegetation: disas, bulbs, succulents, ferns, pelargoniums (the stock from which geraniums have been hybridized

A SUMMER GARDEN

The gardens of **Kirstenbosch** are attractive all year round but are best in spring (September and October), when the annuals and many proteas are in bloom, and the bird life at its most animated.

Jazz and other concerts enliven summer Sunday evenings. Guided tours are offered during the week. The gardens have been recently enhanced by an impressive new Visitor's Centre, incorporating an information office, book-and-souvenir shop, restaurant, and modern Glass House conservatory.

Above: *The floral delights of Kirstenbosch.*
Below: *Proteas feature strongly in the Garden.*
Opposite: *A refreshing halt on the drive through the scenic Constantia area.*

to decorate the window-boxes of five continents) and the fascintating, primeval cycads (*see* p. 8).

The greater proportion of this floral wealth can be seen in the relatively small (160ha; 395 acres) cultivated section. Of special note is the **Cycad Ampitheatre**; sanctuary for most of southern Africa's 20-odd species (falling into two genera) of a plant type that first appeared 150 million years ago to reach its ascendancy about 80 million years later, during the last age of the dinosaurs (*see* p. 8).

The cultivated area is logically arranged in a series of informal spreads that include, among much else, the **Protea Gardens** and the succulents of the **J.W. Matthews Rock Garden**. Meandering between these specialized sections are pathways that invite the leisurely stroller. For the visually disabled, there's a **perfume garden** and a **braille walk**.

Of modest historical interest are the remains of a wild-almond hedge planted in 1660 (to keep the first Dutch settlement's cattle stock from being stolen), and a charming little pool; built with Batavian brick, in the shape of a bird.

Kirstenbosch is primarily a research centre; intense study and meticulous documentation are undertaken in the on-site **Compton**

Herbarium, repository of more than 250,000 botanical specimens. Some of the items belong to now-extinct species.

Constantia Nek ★★

The scenic route along **Rhodes Avenue** (M63) from Kirstenbosch up to Constantia Nek – the summit of a pass that links the Hout Bay and Constantia valleys – is a visual joy, as the road winds through a fantasia of trees, ferns and flowers. On your right is the **Cecilia forest** which is popular among Capetonian walkers, ramblers and those who feel the need to commune with gentler spirits. The waterfall is worth beating a path to.

At the top of the Nek (where there's a pleasant eaterie), the route divides: the road to the right leading to Hout Bay (*see* p. 55), that to the left taking you down into Constantia proper and its three time-honoured and graceful Cape Dutch homesteads.

Groot Constantia ★★★

The lime-washed, gabled and beautifully thatched mansion, perhaps the country's stateliest, was originally conceived and built, and its first vineyards laid out, in 1685 by Cape governor **Simon van der Stel** (*see* p. 13), who happily spent his declining years there. His ghost, it is said, still walks the oak-lined avenue that leads to an ornamental pool where the local aristocracy once disported themselves.

> ### ELEGANCE AT ALPHEN
>
> An historic **Constantia** homestead that does not feature on the formal 'wine route', but is well worth visiting, is **Alphen**, located on an estate first farmed in 1714. The stately double-storeyed Cape Dutch house, which dates from 1753, now functions as a country hotel noted for its superbly proportioned rooms, high beamed ceilings leaded-light windows and its wealth of antiques, oil paintings and objets d'art. Some of the guest rooms open out onto pleasant courtyards. **The Winery** is a showpiece, the cellar is well-stocked with award-winning vintages. The Boer and the Brit is the cozy pub.

In 1778 Groot Constantia was bought by the wealthy Cloete family, who had an eye for beauty as well as a gift for wine making (Constantia products were praised by, among others, Napoleon, Bismarck and Louis Philippe of France). In 1791 **Hendrik Cloete**, the patriarch, added a splendid two-storeyed cellar designed by the French architect Louis Thibault. Its pediment is decorated by sculptor Anton Anreith with a stucco relief of Ganymede, cup-bearer to the Grecian gods, and a bevy of cavorting cherubs.

TASTING TIMES

• **Groot Constantia:** markets about 15 wines. Tastings, sales. Tours are held hourly between 10:00 and 17:00 every day of the year except Christmas Day and Good Friday; tel: 794-5128. Restaurants: **Jonkershuis**, tel: 794-6255; **The Tavern**, tel: 794-1144.
• **Klein Constantia:** red and white wines, renowned for its dessert wines. Tastings and sales Monday to Friday 09:00–17:00, Saturday 09:00–13:00; guided tours by appointment; tel: 794-5188.
• **Buitenverwachting:** red and white wines. Tastings and sales Monday to Friday 09:00–17:00; Saturday 09:00–13:00; cellar tours Monday to Saturday at 11:00 and 15:00; tel: 794-5190. The restaurant, one of the Cape's best, is open Monday to Friday for lunch and dinner, Saturday for dinner only; tel: 794-3522.
• **Steenberg:** at present white wines only. Sales by appointment; tel: 713-2211.

The cellar is now a museum that tells the story of wine and wine-making through the ages.

The main house burned down in 1925, but restoration work over the years has been meticulous, and the place still looks very much as it did at the height of its glory. Inside, you'll find period furniture, tapestries, paintings, exquisite porcelain (Delft, Rhineland, Chinese and Japanese) and objets d'art.

Nearby is the **Jonkershuis** (the Dutch word for 'young gentleman's house'), a kind of annex which, in the early days and among the more affluent Dutch landowners, was reserved for the family's eldest son.

Groot Constantia houses two restaurants. Traditional Cape fare is served in the Jonkershuis; the **Tavern** offers buffet lunches, bench seating and a sociable, rather Germanic atmosphere. Many visitors, though, prefer to bring along a picnic hamper and relax on the shade-dappled lawns. A watch-tower gives a bird's-eye view of the vineyards. There are tours of the modern cellar, wine tastings and sales for those who want to invest in a bottle or two, an art gallery and souvenir shop.

The Smaller Homesteads **

Groot Constantia is one of four working estates that, together, comprise the Peninsula's only 'wine route'. More modest but just as eye-catching in its own way is **Klein Constantia**, built in 1796 and rescued from neglect,

and quite beautifully renovated, by Capetonian Douglas Jooste. It's a rather private place, but one can tour the modern cellars (they have won design awards) by appointment and purchase wine. Klein Constantia's Vin de Constance is extremely popular in exclusive French restaurants.

Nearby is **Buitenverwachting** ('beyond expectations'), an impressive complex of gabled house, cellars, slave quarters and stables that have been faultlessly restored. The estate runs one of the Western Cape's best restaurants, and produces some of its most outstanding wines (many releases have won international acclaim). Again, cellar tours are conducted by appointment; tastings and sales are a daily feature.

The oldest of all the farms is **Steenberg**, on the corner of Steenberg and Tokai Roads. Steenberg Farm was granted to Catharina Ras (Ustings) in 1682, the title deed formally signed by Simon van der Stel in 1688. The farm was later owned by Russouws and then the Louws and finally purchased in 1990 by Johannesburg Consolidated Investment Company. Steenberg produces wine of superior quality; visits and sales by appointment.

Silvermine Nature Reserve ★

This pristine, 2000ha (4942 acres) wilderness extends over the **Steenberg hills**, and across the narrow waist of the Peninsula, from **Kalk Bay** and **Muizenberg** in the east to **Noordhoek** in the west. Tranquillity and scenic variety are the drawcards; the terrain is rugged, an attractive compound of mountain peak, plateau and forested gorge, upland stream, waterfall and, everywhere, an astonishing floral diversity. Bird life is prolific.

A network of safe paths has been laid out; charted walks – ranging from a half-hour stroll to a half-day expedition – take in viewsites and picnic spots (many of which you can also drive to). Magnificent coast-to-coast views unfold along the route to the heights above the reservoir.

Silvermine – early Dutch settlers dug the slopes for the precious metal, though without success – is bisected by the scenically entrancing **Ou Kaapse Weg** that leads southwest to Sun Valley. The drive is thoroughly recommended.

THE OLD CAPE ROAD

Ou Kaapse Weg ('Old Cape Road', or the M64) is a fine scenic drive that cuts through the **Silvermine Nature Reserve**, running southwest from the **Westlake** area to climb over the **Steenberg** ('stony mountain') plateau before descending to **Fish Hoek** Valley and **Noordhoek** on the west coast. Along the winding way are a myriad indigenous flowers that are at their colourful best in springtime, and splendid views across the southern Peninsula. Among the most eye-catching vistas is that from just below the entrance to the Silvermine Reserve.

Opposite: *Historic Groot Constantia, oldest and stateliest of the Peninsula's homesteads. Its vineyards, first planted in 1685, continue to yield fine wines.*
Below: *One of many contour paths through Silvermine Nature Reserve.*

6
The Winelands

Beyond the bleak Cape Flats, to the north and east of Cape Town, the land rises to the splendid upland ranges of the coastal rampart. The hills – part of what are known as the Cape fold mountains – are high, their lower slopes and the valleys in between green, fertile, mantled by pastures and orchards and, especially, by vineyards heavy with fruit.

The Winelands were the first of the country areas to be occupied by the early white settlers. As the farmers flourished so they established villages and, from the later 1600s, began enlarging and beautifying their homes. The first houses were modest but, with prosperity, took on wings and cellars, lofts, slave quarters and courtyards.

THE WINE ROUTES
Perhaps the most enjoyable way of exploring this region is via various wine routes – wine-tasting and sightseeing itineraries inspired by and modelled on the successful *weinstrassen* of Germany and France's *routes de vin*.

There are around ten of these wine-ways, collectively covering the ground from the Cape Peninsula (Constantia: *see* p. 73) northeast as far as Worcester and Robertson, east to take in the Little Karoo, and up the western coastal belt, where the Swartland and Olifantsrivier wineries attract an ever-increasing number of visitors. Three routes, however, are pre-eminent in the Winelands proper.

The **Stellenbosch Wine Route** was the first to be established (in 1971) and is the largest: it embraces five

CAPE DUTCH – A UNIQUE STYLE

Cape Dutch architecture is unique in character. It evolved over a century and has many variations. But the Winelands mansions share many common elements: thick, white-washed walls, thatched roofs, and an elegant symmetry of line. The focal point is the imposing central entrance, flanked by evenly-spaced, shuttered windows and sur-mounted by an impressive gable. The front door leads straight into the *voorkamer* (ante room), which is often divided from the *agterkamer* (rear room) by an elaborate, wooden screen (folded to either side for entertaining).

Opposite: *The vineyards of Franschhoek Valley.*

SOME DRINKING PLACES

Stellenbosch, heart of the Winelands and a town enlivened by its large student population, is especially well served by pubs and taverns. Most offer inexpensive pub lunches, some serve full meals, provide live music and stay open till late. Among the more popular are:
- **De Akker**, in Dorp Street. A wine-tasting centre as well as a favourite pub of students.
- **De Kelder**, in Dorp Street. A la carte Austrian cuisine.
- **Jan Cats**, in Andringa Street. Part of the historic Stellenbosch Hotel.
- **Legends**, in Bird Street.
- **O'Hagan's**, also in Bird Street. Traditional Irish pub.
- **Uncle Ben's**, in Andringa Street. American food.

Above: *La Concorde, headquarters of KWV.*
Below: *Indulgent wine tasting at Nederburg.*

co-operative wineries and 23 cellars, many of them centuries old, their Cape Dutch homesteads a delight to the eye. Nearby **Franschhoek**, in the lovely valley of that name, offers 16 venues, most with names reflecting their French Huguenot origins. The **Paarl Vintners** has 23 members and also offers the full spectrum of wines; from light whites to full-bodied reds, ports and sherries – and one or two especially notable venues (including the giant KWV wine enterprise and Nederburg: *see* p. 95).

The wine routes are well signposted with their distinctive emblems. Most of the cellars offer tastings and tours; some run restaurants with sophisticated menus (traditional Cape dishes feature prominently), others offer simple fare of the 'vintner's or cheese platter'; at still others you'll find a small museum, a gallery, a farm stall that sells home-made preserves, fruit and cheeses.

Visitors are cordially received. The growers are proud of their vineyards and vintages, and will talk revealingly of the subtleties and secrets of wine-making. The tours are leisurely affairs during which you take in the bottling and labelling processes and the tiered casks stored away in the dim coolness of a wine- and wood-scented cellar.

STELLENBOSCH ★★★

South Africa's second oldest town, founded in 1679 and named in honour of Simon van der Stel, lies in the green and pleasant Eerste ('first') River valley beneath the heights of the **Papegaaiberg**, or 'parrot mountain'. The place wears its age with grace: the early towns-folk planted oak trees, created open spaces, built churches and charming little lime-washed homes; later generations added statelier private residences, some fine public edifices and a university.

Above: *Quaint Cape farmstead.*

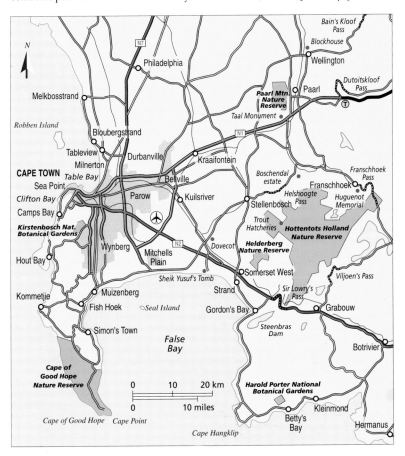

Today, the thoroughfares of the town are still lined
with massive oaks – hence the Afrikaans name 'Eikestad'
('town of oaks'). Much else of the past also remains. The
legacy is strikingly visible in and around the town centre, which embraces around 60 national heritage monuments. Many may be found in **Dorp Street**, which boasts
the country's largest row of historic buildings.

Places from the Past

Four splendid houses, representing different eras, have
been faithfully restored to their original glory and now
form Stellenbosch's **Village Museum**, a complex that
illuminates the changing domestic scene during the 18th
and much of the 19th centuries. Each is furnished in
period fashion, its garden filled with the kinds of plants
– decorative, medicinal and culinary – that the early
owners would have cultivated.

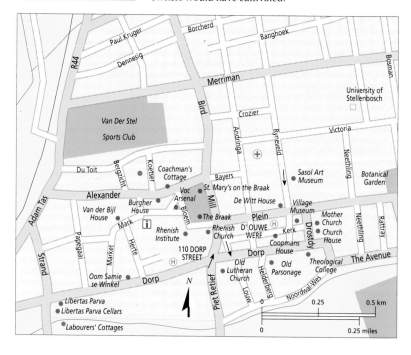

The oldest of the houses is **Schreuderhuis**, built in 1709 by a German immigrant, its architecture, décor and simple, rough-hewn furniture matching his humble status. Much grander is **Blettermanhuis**, which is typical of the late-18th century. **Grosvenor House**, the kind of town house built by patrician Cape families of the early 1800s, is the most elegant of the four, and its garden the most interesting (it houses a permanent exhibition entitled 'Toys of Yesteryear'). Finally there's the home of **O.M. Bergh**, dating from the latter part of the 19th century and Victorian in character.

Above: *The old Kruithuis in Stellenbosch, built as a powder magazine and arsenal in 1777.*

Restoration work is continuing, and the Village Museum is to be enlarged with the addition of two more houses, covering the Edwardian and 1920s periods.

You'll also find some noteworthy buildings around **Die Braak**, the spacious village green that once served both as a parade ground for the militia and as an arena for local festivities. Its military origins are evident in the nearby **Kruithuis** (arsenal), built in 1777 and now a national monument housing old weaponry and Dutch East India Company memorabilia. Other points of interest include the **Burgerhuis** (once the home of the magistrate and now a museum and headquarters of the Historical Homes of South Africa); the delightful little thatch-roofed Anglican church of **St Mary's-on-the-Braak**, and the **Rhenish Mission** complex, whose church pulpit is one of the finest in the country.

In somewhat lighter vein, make a point of calling in at Oom Samie se Winkel, which translates as Uncle Sammy's Shop and which first opened its doors for business during Stellenbosch's infancy. It's since been given a Victorian facelift, complete with wrought-iron tracery, the interior crammed with home-made preserves, bric-a-brac, curios,

---

WALKING THROUGH THE WINELANDS

Hikers and ramblers have a wide choice of routes through the Winelands: from strenuous scrambles over rugged slopes to gentle walks through the fertile farmlands, the **Jonkershoek Valley** and the **Assegaaibosch** and **Helderberg** reserves. Among the most enticing is the **Vineyard Trail**, a marked route that starts from Stellenbosch's **Oude Libertas Centre**, then up the **Papegaaiberg**, through forest plantations, orchards and vineyards to **Kuilsrivier** in the west. The full route is 24km (15 miles) long and takes a day to complete, but you can turn off after 7km (4.5 miles) and return to Stellenbosch through the exquisite **Devon Valley**.

Above: *Oom Samie's shop.*

bottles of good wine and much else. The scents that regale you – of spices and fresh fruit, tobacco, dried fish and leather – belong to that long-gone, more leisurely age before the coming of supermarkets.

Part of **Oom Samie se Winkel** has been set aside as **The Victorian Wine Shop**, a cozy little corner that houses the region's best releases together with some unusual vintages. The staff will make up (and despatch) gift packages for you. There's also a pleasant tea-garden at the back. **De Akker**, a few steps along the road, is a lively pub and popular wine-tasting centre.

One of South Africa's earliest and most attractive inns is **D'Ouwe Werf** ('The Old Yard'), located on Church Street. The hotel has been welcoming guests for close on three centuries, though under different guises, and is a stylish place recently renovated in keeping with its venerable past. The best of the 25 rooms are sumptuously furnished with four-posters, magnificent antiques and opulent fabrics. Its **Koffiehuis** restaurant, which has an entrancing outside area shaded by vine-covered pergolas, serves traditional Cape food, scrumptious home-made cakes, pastries and excellent coffee.

The World of Wine

As you can imagine, Stellenbosch has much to offer the wine-lover. Well worth visiting is **Libertas Parva Cellar**, an elegantly gabled Cape Dutch mansion that houses the massive vats, presses and old implements of the Stellenryck Wine Museum. Especially intriguing exhibits include the ancient Greek and Roman amphora, a jug from Biblical Israel, goblets and bottles from the early Dutch Cape and some fine examples of antique glassware.

Next door, **Libertas Parva**, once home to the wife of statesman Jan Smuts and social venue for many South African political luminaries, has retained its period character. It also houses the well-known **Rembrandt van Rijn Art Museum** of works by some of the country's leading artists.

Some of the world's biggest wine vats can be seen in the coolness of the **Bergkelder**, a labyrinthine cellar complex tunnelled out of Stellenbosch's Papegaaiberg mountain. The cloister-like, candle-lit, aromatic chambers are lined to their arched ceilings with tiered bottles; one section has been set aside as the Vinotèque (a place where wines owned by private individuals – mainly investors – are matured). Tours and tastings are offered.

Above: Oak-lined Dorp Street in Stellenbosch was known as 'the wagon road to the Cape'. It has the country's longest row of historic buildings.

Near Stellenbosch

The **Van Ryn Brandy distillery** and maturation cellars, on the R310 in Vlottenburg Road, to the southwest of town, are among the country's largest and most impressive. Guided tours take in tastings, audio-visuals, cooperage demonstrations and brandy courses are offered, musical evenings are sometimes laid on and, once or twice a year, there's a special 'brandy breakfast' train excursion from Cape Town, with cocktails and a pleasant brunch included in the fare.

Those interested in fine craft will delight in a visit to the nearby **Jean Craig pottery** (it's on the Devon Valley road), where you stand in the central area and watch the potters at work. Styles vary from the simple to the sophisticated; the designs are imaginative, the general quality excellent. Craftwork of an entirely different kind

HEALTH HYDRO

If the good food and wine of the region threatens to take its toll, pay a visit to **High Rustenberg Hydro** in the attractive Ida's Valley near Stellenbosch. Among South Africa's premier health resorts, the hydro offers an invigorating and individually monitored regimen of massage, hydro- and heat-therapy, water aerobics and much else, all enjoyed in luxurious surrounds.

You really need to stay for a week or more to extract maximum benefit from the routine and treatments, but the Hydro also caters for day visitors in search of a briefer stress-free retreat.

Light lunches (salad buffet) are served; booking essential; tel: (021) 883-8600.

Map showing the Stellenbosch winelands region, with locations including Klapmuts, Simonsvlei, Drakenstein, Muldersvlei, Koelenhof, Backsberg, Lievland, Simondium, Villiera, Simonsig, Kannonkop, Kraaifontein, Muratie, Delheim, Koelenhof, Morgenhof, Schoongezicht, Bottelary, Hartenberg, Bertrams, Banhoek, Delaire, Uiterwyk, Neethlingshof, Stellenbosch, Goedgeloof, Vlottenburg, Zevenwacht, Eersterivier, Valfei, Brandy Cellar, Blaauwklippen, Lynedoch, Spier, Hottentots Holland Nature Reserve, Welmoed, Rust en Vrede, Eikendal, De Helderberg, Helderberg Nature Reserve, Firgrove, Macassar, Macassar Beach, Somerset West. Roads: N1, N2, R44, R304, R310, M12, M23. Scale: 0–4 km / 0–2.5 miles.

Below: *The traditional Cape Dutch interior of Blaauwklippen Manor.*
Opposite left: *The Delaire homestead.*
Opposite right: *Wooded hills and vineyards embrace the Morgenhof estate.*

is on view at **Dombeya Farm** (off the R44 near Rust-en-Vrede wine estate), a worthwhile community weaving project that turns out colourful fabrics, mats, shawls and jerseys, made from locally spun wool.

THE STELLENBOSCH WINE FARMS ***

The 28 cellars and co-operatives on the Stellenbosch wine route are all located on four major roads within a 12km (7 miles) radius of the town. Each one is well worth visiting for its wines, its ambience and the charm of its setting. Among the more prominent wine farms are:

Blaauwklippen, a classic H-shaped Cape Dutch mansion with intricately decorative

gables. It's also a working, all-purpose farm. Among its eclectic attractions is a museum of coaches, carriages, vintage and veteran vehicles. During the summer months, there are tours of the vineyards by horse-drawn coach and a delicious and sustaining 'coachman's lunch' is available at a reasonable price.

Delaire, situated high up on the Helshoogte pass, offers a small range of wines, lunches at the Green Door restaurant, picnics on the lawns in season and splendid views.

Delheim, a long-time stalwart on the wine route is situated on the slopes of the Simonsberg. With good wines, alfresco eating and memorable vistas across to Table Mountain and the coast, Delheim's tasting room is a place for lingering.

Eikendal is on the Somerset West road, on the slopes of the Helderberg mountains. Quality classic wines from the Austrian- and SA-trained team. Daily lunches, based on Swiss country cuisine. Friday evening Swiss-cheese fondues are a winter speciality.

Hartenberg, on the Botttelary road, offers an impressive line-up of wines from a young, dynamic team. Vintners lunches daily (except Sunday). Tastings and sales.

Hazendal, here a predominantly female team are busily shaping this estate's future direction. A new cellar sports the latest in technology, while the old cellar has become the tasting centre. Wine and music evenings at the restaurant in winter.

Morgenhof, on the R44, dates from 1692, the homestead from 1820. French-owned by the Huchon family, owners of Gosset champagne (est. 1584). New vineyards, barrel-maturation cellar for whites and underground octagonal barrel cellar for reds all add up to an estate dedicated to quality. Light lunches all year round, picnics in summer.

Muratie, a fine Cape Dutch homestead, one of the region's oldest, (est. 1685), is noted for its ports and red wines. Cellar tours by appointment.

Neethlingshof has a beautiful avenue of stone pines leading to a showpiece estate whose drawcards include the Lord Neethling restaurant and the more casual, glass-enclosed Palm Terrace. The gabled house is famed for its exquisite grounds. Tastings and sales daily, farm tours with braai in summer, cellar tours on request.

Saxenburg, leading proponent of 'new wave' Cape wines, situated on the slopes of the Bottelary Hill above Kuilsrivier. Range includes an SA-French blend, from grapes

SPIER WINE ESTATE

This estate has recently been renovated and upgraded into a showpiece for the Cape winelands. Attractions include wine tastings, a wine shop and a range of eating options (try the Taphuis pub, lighter meals at Café Spier, or more traditional fare in the Jonkershuis Restaurant). Picnic baskets are also for sale and visitors can wander the attractive grounds, or take a trip in an old horse-drawn cart. There are pony rides for children.
The open air amphitheatre offers live jazz, classical and light music in summer.
A cheetah breeding project forms part of the property, as do stables. For a full day's outing, take the Spier Express train, departing from the V&A Waterfront on Wednesdays and Saturdays.

Below: *Trout hatcheries in enchanting Jonkershoek.*
Opposite: *The Huguenot Memorial, Franschhoek.*

grown on the owner's properties in both countries. Tastings (Mon-Sat) are charged for. The Guinea Fowl restaurant offers lunch (Wed-Mon) and dinner.

Simonsig is located between Stellenbosch and the N1. It comprises three original farms, dating to 1682. One of the largest Cape estates and the first in SA to produce a *méthode champenoise* sparkling wine . Cellar tours Monday to Saturday. Tasting is charged for.

Uiterwyk has been in the same family since 1912. The homestead, built in 1791, is a national monument. Cellar tours by appointment.

Welmoed is on the R310 and the first winery on the route when approached from the N2. Cellar tours by appointment, but excellent wine tasting and sales. The restaurant offers wholesome and filling lunches.

JONKERSHOEK VALLEY **

The **Eerste River** rises to the east of Stellenbosch, and flows through a hill-flanked countryside that beckons the hiker and lover of nature. Within the valley are the historic homesteads of **Oude Nektar** and **Lanzerac**; the latter is a neo-Classical manor-house that made its appearance in 1830 (though some of the outbuildings are much older) and which is now one of the region's best-known hotels. Guests approach the beautifully maintained complex along an avenue of stately plane trees. The outhouses have been converted into bedrooms, the original wine-cellar into the reception area and fine restaurant. Lanzerac also houses the informal Vinkel en Koljander restaurant, an art gallery and a small museum of Cape furniture.

Stellenbosch university's **Jonkershoek Fisheries Research Station**, which runs South Africa's oldest and largest hatcheries,

breeds trout, bream and bass for release into rivers and dams throughout the country. The aquarium features local and some exotic freshwater fish species.

Some 160ha (395 acres) of precious Cape mountain *fynbos* (heath-type) vegetation are protected within the valley's **Assegaaibosch Nature Reserve**. A variety of the proteas are both rare and eye-catching. A network of short walks has been laid out, together with picnic and barbecue sites and a small (5ha; 12 acres) wildflower garden with specimens labelled for identification.

Further to the east is the much larger (400ha; 988 acres) **Hottentots Holland Nature Reserve**, a splendid area of mountains, gorges, dense woodlands and tumbling upland streams. This is a place for serious walkers (there's no access for cars), many of whom embark on the challenging Boland trail, a three-day, 41km (25 miles) route divided into shorter circular sections. If you're interested in wild flowers, keep an eye out for the rare marsh rose and the blushing bride. For the rest, there are forest-clad kloofs to explore, clear mountain pools to bathe in, and superb views over the countryside towards the coast.

FRANSCHHOEK ★★★

The town's name – it means 'French corner' – reflects its Gallic origins: it was founded in 1688 by a party of **Huguenot** *emigres*, refugees from a Europe torn by the religious wars. There were not very many of them, and they were scattered among the resident Dutch and German freeburghers rather than allowed to form a separate community, so they soon lost their language and cultural identity. But they were hard-working and skilled folk, and they did much for the local wine industry – and the architecture of

---

SOME COMMON CULTIVARS

WHITE
- **Chardonnay:** the grape of the world's great white wines.
- **Sauvignon blanc:** SA's best white cultivar, made in new world and French styles.
- **Chenin blanc:** versatile workhorse making a range from dry to botrytis dessert wines. Also called Steen.
- **Colombard:** easy drinking varietal, also used for brandy.
- **Muscat d'Alexandre:** sweet, heavy mainly dessert wines. Also called Hanepoot.

RED
- **Cabernet Sauvignon:** this classic varietal is widely planted. New and old world styles are made.
- **Pinotage:** SA's 'own' varietal is now achieving fame world-wide.
- **Shiraz:** known for its fine flavour and 'smoky' bouquet.
- **Merlot:** Gaining strength as a stand-alone varietal.
- **Cinsaut:** Used mainly for blending or light easy wines.

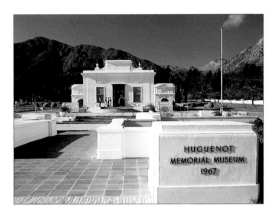

FRANCHHOEK FOOD

- **Chez Michel:** traditional Continental dishes served in a bistro setting.
- **Die Binnehof:** a wine house girded by lawns, trees and rose-beds; Provençal platter lunches; big picnic baskets; cosy bistro-type meals in winter.
- **La Maison de Chamonix:** on the Chamonix estate; French food; Sunday buffet; picnics on the lawns.
- **La Petite Ferme:** simple, country-style fare (fresh or smoked trout a speciality) and spectacular views of the Franschhoek Valley.
- **Le Ballon Rouge:** French food, using the freshest of homegrown ingredients.
- **Le Quartier Francais:** award-winning restaurant serving a blend of Cape Malay and Provençal dishes in a simple but elegant setting.
- **Polfyntjies:** country-style Cape and other dishes served in a garden setting.

Above : *Franschhoek's early settlers remembered.*
Below: *Strawberry fields.*

the region. As a legacy of their Huguenot past, many fine estates and homesteads still bear their original French names, among them **La Provence**, **La Motte**, **Haute Provence**, **La Couronne** and **L'Ormarins**.

The early French Huguenots and their legacy are commemorated in a very imposing, though delicately graceful, memorial and museum complex in Franschhoek. The monument is full of elaborate Christian symbolism – three elegant arches represent the Holy Trinity; a female figure holds a Bible and a broken chain (Freedom of Religion) and is casting off her cloak (of Oppression); the fleurs-de-lis on her dress indicates Nobility and she straddles a miniature earth (Liberty of Spirit). The museum, a leading centre of research into Huguenot origins and culture, houses antique Cape furniture, silverware and early farm implements. Many Afrikaans surnames like Jordaan, Le Roux, Malan and Theron can be traced here.

Franschhoek, set among the vineyards of the lovely valley, is a pleasant little town that draws its prosperity from the surrounding wine and fruit farms (the area gave birth to South Africa's flourishing fruit export industry and it is part of the **Four Passes Fruit Route**, *see* p. 98). It is also a culinary mecca; its award-winning restaurants catering for a devoted clientele of national and international gourmets.

Food and wine, too, are good reasons for visiting nearby **Boschendal**, a graceful, old Cape Flemish style mansion and centrepiece of extensive vineyards. The restaurant here is famed for its traditional Cape buffet lunches; the old tap-house (taphuis) serves as a tasting room; much of the rest of the house is of museum standard. On offer are tours of the estate, picnics, wine tastings and sales.

Boschendal is a member of the **Vignerons de Franschhoek,** an association established to promote the area's wines and wineries. Some may be visited by appointment only, but all their products can be sampled at the co-operative wine centre in town.

Bellingham, an old (1693) farm that suffered decades of neglect, is now one of the region's most respected wine producers. Its cellar complex is especially impressive; (wine tastings are provided) concerts are sometimes staged in its intimate (90-seat) amphitheatre.

Cabrière Estate, overlooking the valley, specialises in the production of Cap Classique, the name by which the Cape's sparkling wines made in the champagne method are known. The underground cellar is worth a visit.

L'Ormarins is a stunningly attractive, gabled house overlooking a large ornamental pond. The cellar is old and atmospheric, its equipment high-tech.

La Motte, another estate that can trace its origins to the Huguenots, produces red wines of excellent quality.

Franschhoek Vineyards Co-operative produces wine, from grapes supplied by its members, mainly under the La Cotte label. Some of the profits have been devoted to the restoration of the La Cotte mill, built in 1779. Tours are arranged by appointment.

Franschhoek Mountain Manor is a luxury hotel and conference centre, while the buildings of the adjacent **Swiss Farm Excelsior** timeshare complex are designed in Alpine style, with sloping roofs, quaint weathervanes and bright-flowered window boxes.

> ### TOURING WITH A DIFFERENCE
>
> Most visitors see the winelands by car, on conducted tours, or on foot along some of the pleasant walking trails. There are, though, some less conventional ways of exploring this scenic and interest-filled region, among them:
>
> ● **On horseback:** A number of tour operators offer horse trail excursions. Contact Captour.
>
> ● **By helicopter:** (with wine tasting and a lunch included): contact Court Helicopters, tel: (021) 25-2966, Civair, tel: (021) 419-5182. Some operators fly to Franschhoek and further; ask Captour for details.
>
> ● **By hot-air balloon:** (plus champagne) contact Wineland Ballooning, Paarl, tel: (02211) 863-3192.
>
> ● **By water:** Several enterprises cater for rafting and canoeing enthusiasts, including Breede River Adventures; tel: (021) 683-6433.

SOMERSET WEST ★★

This fast-growing town occupies the southern part of the Stellenbosch winelands, flanked by **False Bay** and the lofty **Hottentots Holland** mountains in the east. To cross these massive ramparts, you wind your way up the dizzy heights of **Sir Lowry's Pass**.

Among the attractions of the area is the **Helderberg Nature Reserve**, a 400ha (988 acres) expanse of heath and indigenous forest (yellowwood, stinkwood and ironwood trees are prominent) set beneath the high and often cloud-wreathed Helderberg peak.

Right: *Vergelegen, home to an early Cape governor.*
Opposite: *The graceful Afrikaans Language Monument at Paarl.*

From the summit there are spectacular views of sea and mountain, vineyards and rolling farmlands. The plant life, which includes some rare proteas, was devastated by fire in 1994 but fynbos' powers of recovery are legendary and the outlook is good.

Starting from the reserve's entrance are several walks, the longest leading to the lovely **Disa Gorge** where, in late summer, a profusion of wild flowers decorates the slopes. Here, too, you'll find a refreshing waterfall.

The Helderberg is sanctuary for a delightful array of birds, including the protea seed-eater (a species unique to the area) and, in the higher reaches, the black eagle, peregrine falcon and mountain buzzard. Among visitor amenities is a shady picnic site, which embraces a herbarium, and a tea-room (open at weekends).

One of the country's earliest and grandest mansions also lies at the foot of the Hottentots Holland range. **Vergelegen** – the name means 'situated faraway', an indication of its one-time remoteness from Cape Town – was built at staggering cost by the eccentric and spendthrift governor Willem Adriaan van der Stel in 1701, and within a few years became lavishly girded by vineyards (half a million vines were planted), orchards and pastures. Such showy wealth outraged the local farmers, who complained bitterly of unfair trading competition. More serious was Van der Stel's scandalous use of official (Dutch East India Company) money, materials and slave labour in the creation of the estate, and in due course he was removed from office.

Vergelegen, like so many other historic homesteads, suffered decades of mistreatment and neglect but was eventually bought (in 1917) and restored by the magnate

---

TREES OF THE HELDERBERG

The majestic yellowwood and stinkwood trees found in the **Helderberg Nature Reserve** produce close-grained timber that has been fashioned into some of the finest of Cape furniture. Most of the pieces are now valuable antiques. The two most common yellowwood species are the Outeniqua, which grows to 60m (nearly 200ft) in height, and the 'real' yellowwood, the most widely distributed. Three unrelated trees bear the name stinkwood, of which the black stinkwood is the most sought-after. The red stinkwood, or bitter almond, was used in wagon-making and for domestic purposes. The hardwood forests that once covered much of the southern coastal region were depleted by early settlers, and the species are now strictly protected.

Sir Lionel Phillips and his wife Florence. Thirty years later it hosted an appreciative British Royal Family and Queen Elizabeth II visited it again in 1995. It now belongs to the giant Anglo American group, and is open to the public.

The house itself is ochre-walled, thatch-roofed and splendidly gabled; the interior light, airy, filled with fine furniture, including Bayeux tapestries and an especially

beautiful teak and yellowwood screen. A recent addition is the octagonal, four-level winery (partly underground); the first products of which were released in 1992.

The surrounding grounds are a 'lotion for the eyes', their focal point the Octagonal Garden, originally used for holding livestock and now a fantasia of wrought-iron trellises, wide herbaceous borders and flowering plants (more than 300 kinds). Especially notable are Vergelegen's trees, among them five camphors planted in 1700, a rare Dawn redwood (once thought to be extinct) and what is believed to be South Africa's oldest oak. There is public access to part of the house, to the **Lady Phillips Restaurant and Tea Garden**, to the interpretive centre, the lovely Octagonal and Rose gardens and winery.

THE BERG AND BREEDE RIVER VALLEYS *

Majestic mountain ranges flank the course of the Berg River as it winds its way to the Atlantic. For a small part of the way it graces the **Perelvallei** – the 'vale of pearls' that takes its name from **Paarl Mountain** which, with its three distinctively shaped rocks, reminded an early Dutch explorer of a cluster of pearls, especially as the dawn sunlight glistened on the rounded, mica-studded surfaces. Beneath lies Paarl, largest of the region's towns.

To the north is the **Breede river,** which rises in the Ceres basin to flow southeast, nurturing a countryside of vineyards and orchards.

Paarl **

The town is noted for some impressive old buildings, for a 11km (7 miles) long main street ornamented with jacarandas and oaks, for its prominent role in the wine industry and its close associations with the long, and often controversial, campaign for the recognition of the Afrikaans language (taal). On the slopes of the mountain stands the **Taal Monument**, an impressive structure of three linked columns, fountain and soaring spire. Each of these elements symbolizes a debt owed by the language – to the Western world, to the slaves brought in from the East, and to Africa.

The mountain – which you can drive up via a circular road – is the centrepiece of the **Paarlberg Nature Reserve**, sanctuary for proteas and other *fynbos* plants, wild olives, orchids and patches of natural forest. Hiking paths, barbecue and picnic spots have been laid out; the small dams of the area are much favoured by serious anglers for the unusually large black bass they sustain.

On the way to the summit you will pass the **Mill Water Wild Flower Garden**. Do make a brief digression, especially if you're visiting in springtime (August and September), when great carpets of yellow, orange and red blooms cover the slopes.

From the top of **Paarl Rock** – where there's an old cannon, a beacon and a cave – one can take in the glory of the Berg River valley, its towering walls and, in the distance, Table Mountain and the ocean.

In Taillefert Street is **Laborie**, a handsome old manor house and model wine estate that offers tours (by arrangement) and a restaurant serving classic Cape fare. Laborie is owned by the **KWV** (Ko-operatieve Wijnbouwers Vereniging), the world's largest cellar complex under one roof, whose massive wine and brandy

---

Weaving Magic

Bhabhathane is the Xhosa word for 'butterfly', symbolizing the colourful success of this self-help weaving scheme. It was launched in the mid-1980s in a desperate effort to beat the local unemployment crisis, and now turns out a range of handmade items, including runners, carpets and tapestries made from mohair and karakul wool. If you don't fancy what's on offer, just sketch your preference and the craftspersons will translate the design into a specially-made woven product. The shop is in Verster Street, Paarl, or you can visit the studio at the Ikwhezi centre, Dal Josafat, on the R303.

Right: *The distinctively rounded bulk of Paarl Rock.*

cellar in Paarl's Kohler Street lays on tastings and tours taking in the famed cathedral cellar with its vaulted roof and large wooden maturation vats. Spare a glance for the company's headquarters, the imposing **La Concorde** mansion on Main Street.

Worth part of your time is the Wagonmakers Museum, which houses displays of a once-flourishing trade (Paarl was a kind of final staging post for treks into the great interior) and the **Oude Pastorie**, originally the church parsonage and now a museum of Cape furniture, silverware, copperware and relics of early colonial settlement.

Other places of interest are **La Bonheur crocodile farm**, with over a thousand of these giant reptiles, (the gift shop stocks some appealing leatherwork), and the **Bhabhathane Community Project** which produces handwoven goods.

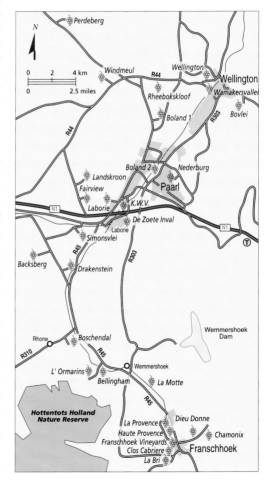

The Paarl Wine Farms ***

Grandest of these farms is **Nederburg**, an elaborately gabled, classic Cape country homestead set in the wide, vineyard-mantled sweep of the **Klein Drakenstein** area to the east of Paarl. The old estate was taken over in the 1937 by the Graue family; refugees from an increasingly hostile Germany.

The Graues, winemakers supreme, soon elevated Nederburg to the top rank of local producers. Now owned by **Stellenbosch Farmers' Winery**, the 24th Nederburg wine auction was held in 1998. This is South Africa's premier annual wine auction, an occasion noted as much for

PLACE OF GOATS

Unusual among winelands estates is **Fairview**, between the R44 and R102 near **Paarl**, which is noted not only for its wines but also for its farm animals, including a herd of Swiss Saanen goats whose milk yields a variety of fine cheeses. A unique feature is the estate's 'goat tower'; a slender, two-storeyed, conical loft which the goats enter and leave via a circular, wooden, outside stairway.

Among other farmyard residents are sheep, pigs, chickens, guineafowl, peacocks, pheasants and quails. Fairview offers wine and cheese tasting, daily except Sundays, between 08:30 and 18:00 (17:00 on Saturdays).

its sociability as for the fine and rare vintages on offer. Merchants, investors, collectors and others with invitations come from all corners to enjoy the sales, the tastings, the fashion show, the excellent lunch. During the rest of the year there are cellar tours (by appointment) that take in tastings and an audio-visual presentation; picnic lunches are served between November and March.

Another lively feature on the Paarl calendar is the annual Nouveau Festival held in April – a glorified street party to which the area's winemakers bring their new products in an eccentric variety of conveyances. Food and wine stalls, music and general merrymaking are the order of the day.

The more prominent of Paarl's wine venues are:

Fairview has excellent vintages, goat's cheese is famous.
Landskroon which is nearby is also known for its cheeses, from the estate's prize-winning Jersey cattle herd.
Backsberg is on the slopes of the Simonsberg. It has an especially atmospheric tasting parlour and a small wine museum. Closed-circuit television helps you along the self-guided cellar tour.
Zandwijk is South Africa's only kosher winery. Cellar tours by arrangement; children love to visit for the farmyard, and for the donkey rides.

At **Paarl Rock Brandy Cellar** in Paarl visitors can view the entire distillation production process; also on offer is an audio-visual presentation, a small museum and tastings.

WELLINGTON *

This attractive little town, just to the north of Paarl, is the centre of a flourishing wine-producing region and headquarters of South Africa's **dried-fruit industry**. If you're passing through, take time out to enjoy the lovely roses in **Victoria Park**. A number of charming Cape Dutch manor-houses can be seen in the general vicinity, including **Twistniet** (the original homestead around which Wellington grew), **Versailles**, **Leliefontein** and **Welvanpas**.

The area's most striking feature is the 30km (20 miles) **Bain's Kloof Pass**, over which the R303 highway makes its way northeastward from town. Motorists en route are treated to spectacular views, and there's a pleasant picnic spot at the summit, after which you descend to the Breede River valley through a countryside of ravines, waterfalls and the dramatic rock formations of the **Wolvenskloof** ('hyena's pass').

THE CERES AREA **

Named after the Roman goddess of agriculture, the pretty little town of Ceres lies in a mountain-fringed basin that is famous for its **fruit orchards** and yields magnificent harvests of apples and pears, peaches, nectarines, cherries, oranges and potatoes. The local fruit-packing plant is the southern hemisphere's largest.

The upland air here is crisp and clean (even in high summer), the scenery superb, the backing hills snow-clad in winter which attract skiers to their slopes. In a nutshell, Ceres is an inviting destination for the get-away-from-it-all weekender, who has a selection of reasonably priced hotels and family resorts to choose from.

Specific features of note include the **Transport Riders' Museum**, where you can see an array of wagons, carts, equipment and utensils used by the early and ruggedly independent overland traders; and the **Ceres Nature Reserve**, whose heath-type flora include some rare species.

For driving interest, take the road southwest over **Michell's Pass**, a cleft in the towering and otherwise impenetrable highland range through which the main

> **MEN WHO MADE TRACKS**
>
> **Michell's Pass** is one of many remarkable engineering feats accomplished by the two Bains, 19th-century South Africa's leading road-builders. Between them, **Andrew Geddes Bain** and his son **Thomas** carved out some of the most challenging routes through the country's southern mountain barrier, creating highways into the great interior that are still used, extensively, today. They include the **Bain's Kloof**, **Michell's**, the precipitous **Katberg**, the **Prince Alfred's**, **Cogman's Kloof** and the magnificent **Swartberg** passes and the cliff-hugging Sea Point–Hout Bay route named **Victoria Drive**. The Bains had other talents, too. Andrew Geddes was a pioneer geologist, respected fossil-hunter and writer. Thomas surveyed railway lines, charted important mineral deposits and established the Orange River's potential for irrigation.

Opposite: *The Andrew Murray Monument outside the N.G. Kerk, Wellington.*
Left: *Ceres transformed into a winter wonderland.*

TOURING THE ORCHARDS

A splendid introduction to the Ceres-Tulbagh area is the **Fruit Route**, in which farmers, co-operatives, farm stalls and packing houses combine to provide an insight into an industry that produces apples and peaches, pears, cherries, nectarines and dried fruit. Tours last anything from a couple of hours to two days. A typical longer excursion will include a coach trip from the city, refreshments and lunch at a farm or hotel, visits to an orchard (there are also 'orchard trails'), a fruit-drying yard and a nature reserve, a tour of the harvesting and packing processes, and an overnight stay on a farm. Captour at the Tourism Gateway has brochures and information, or contact local information offices (Ceres, Tulbagh, Wellington and Wolseley).

Below: *Tulbagh's historic Church Street.*
Opposite: *A candlemaker in action at Kleinplasie.*

road to the interior once ran. The route is marvellously scenic. Further to the east are the precipitous sandstone cliffs and ravines of the **Hex River mountains**, a magnet for climbers and, in winter, for skiers. The valley below is broad, flat, incredibly fertile, sustaining nearly 200 farms that produce most of the country's late-maturing export grapes. The Hex River valley is beautiful in all seasons, but especially so in autumn and early winter when the green land changes to a chequerboard of soft browns and golds.

TULBAGH *

As attractive as Ceres but in quite a different way, is Tulbagh, founded around the Old Church (built in 1745) to grow into a small frontier settlement of graceful public edifices and private homes. Many of these were destroyed in the great earthquake of 1969 – a rare occurrence in South Africa. The convulsion measured 6.5 on the Richter scale, shook the whole of the northern winelands and killed nine people.

In due course the historic and fragile buildings were restored – meticulously so – most of them to a pristine condition they hadn't enjoyed for generations (the once-lovely facades had been ruined by decades of tasteless 'improvements'). In **Church Street** alone there are more than 30 considered important and handsome enough to merit status as national monuments.

Most notable of them, perhaps, is the **Old Church** (timber galleries, fine furniture and paintings) and other elements of the **Volksmuseum complex**. These include **Mon Bijou** (designed by the celebrated Louis Thibault, and today the home of a leading antique collector); the **Victorian House** and, especially, the **Old Drostdy**.

This last served as home to the local landdrost, or magistrate, and is yet another Thibault creation. A superb building, splendidly furnished, it now does duty as museum (early Cape domestic displays), art gallery and headquarters of a major wine company. Visitors are welcomed with a companionable glass of sherry in the old jail-cells before touring the house.

WORCESTER *

The Breede River valley's largest town is noted mainly for its large showgrounds and museum complex, most intriguing component of which is the **Kleinplasie** open-air exposition. Located a short distance outside town, this is a permanent re-creation of the life and times of the Dutch farming pioneers; on display are replicas of cottages and huts, horse mill, coach house, butchery, blacksmith's, domestic kitchen, wine cellar and *witblitz* ('white lightning': a lethal local concoction made of peaches) still, lime kiln, tobacco shed, milk room and much else. There's also an agricultural exhibition hall; a village is in process of reconstruction.

Kleinplasie is very much a 'living museum'; your visit is enlivened by demonstrations of wheat milling, blacksmithing, candle-making, bread-making, tobacco rolling and other sturdy frontier skills. Seasonal programmes take in weaving, spinning, raisin-making, brandy distilling and threshing. A steam train takes visitors on nostalgic trips; wines and local delicacies – cheeses, honey, confectionery, preserves, jams – are displayed on and sold from the stalls of an adjacent country market. The Kleinplasie farmstead incorporates a taproom and restaurant.

Other interesting elements of the Worcester museum complex include the **Afrikaner Museum** (the turn-of-the-century doctor's surgery draws the eye), and **Hugo Naudé House**, where works of this respected South African artist are on view.

Worcester lies on the edge of the Little Karoo, in a transitional zone noted for its fascinating plant life. The local flora and a wealth of other dryland species – bulbs, succulents, carrion flowers, the weird welwitschia, the halfmens and kokerboom trees among them – can be seen in

---

STRONG DRINK

During the early days distilling was a popular home industry in rural villages and on the farms. The rough-and-ready stills produced powerful **brandy-type liquors** variously known as *mampoer*, *witblits* ('white lightning') and *withond* ('white dog'). Basic ingedients ranged from peaches and grapes to potatoes, sugarcane, prickly pears and karee berries. The practice has all but died out – no new licences have been issued in the Western Cape for years – but it remains something of a tourist attraction in the country's northern regions (the Marico-Zeerust area boasts a **Mampoer Route** and annual **Mampoer Festival**). Early stills are on display at a number of venues, including the **Kleinplasie** complex at Worcester.

the **Karoo National Botanic Garden** to the north of town. The 150ha (370 acres) area embraces a 10ha (25 acres) cultivated section where plants are grouped according to type, region and climate. The International Organization for Succulents ranks the reserve as one of the world's five authentic succulent gardens.

OVERNIGHTING IN THE WINELANDS

The region is exceptionally well served by hotels and, especially, by intimate little country lodges, some of them time-honoured farmsteads that pride themselves on their comfort, cuisine and friendly service.

Stellenbosch has its delightful **D'Ouwe Werf** (*see* p. 84) and, in the centre of town, the small and quite beautifully appointed **Stellenbosch Hotel** (architecture, décor and furnishings are a charming stylistic mix of Cape Dutch and Victorian; some of the rooms are furnished with antiques).

In the countryside nearby is the atmospherically English-country **Devon Valley Protea Hotel**, popular for its terrace lunches and lovely gardens. Recently revamped, it is a tranquil haven from which to explore the winelands. The historic **Lanzerac Hotel**, mentioned on page 88, also has its modern offerings., including luxurious suites and conference facilities. The Terrace Restaurant serves light meals, or you can lunch in the 'Governer's Hall', where Cape Malay dishes and Lanzerac's long-established cheese buffet are served from Monday to Friday. Enjoy an English-style high tea on weekends only.

In Paarl and its surrounds you'll find luxury and superb food at the **Grande Roche Hotel** (its **Bosman's** restaurant wins a lot of honours) and at a number of smaller, less formal venues. Among the

WINE EXPORTERS
To send a bottle, case or container load of wine home or abroad, there are experts who will do it for you - safely, with the minimum of hassle and at a reasonable cost.
• **The Wine Warehouse**, Woodstock, (021) 448-0242.
• **Vaughan Johnson Wine Shop**, Waterfront, tel (021) 419-2121.
• **The Vineyard Connection**, Woodstock, tel: (021) 462-3487.
• **Oom Samie se Winkel** Stellenbosch (Victorian Wine Shop), tel: (021) 887-2612.
• **Steven Rom** Sea Point, Cape Town, tel: (021) 439-6043 or 434-0410.
• **Wine-Of-The-Month-Club** Alphen, Constantia, tel: (021) 794-5019.
• **Picardi Fine Wine and Spirits,** Foreshore, Cape Town, tel: (021) 25-1639 or 25-1664.

Left: *The splendid 18th-century Lanzerac homestead now functions as an hotel.*

latter are **Goedemoed Country Inn**, a fine old Cape homestead set on a small estate graced by shady trees, smooth green lawns and beds of roses. The place, although commercially run, still has the feel of a well-loved private home; the antique-filled lounge remains a family room where guests gather in the evening to chat and sip a convivial glass of South African wine.

Similar in some respects is **Mountain Shadows**, which has its own vineyard and whose ten comfortable rooms are divided between the old wine-cellar area, the **Jonkershuis** (traditional home of the heir to the estate) and the main house.

WORLD OF SNAKES

The most recent addition to **Worcester's** Kleinplasie Open-air Museum Complex is **Reptile World**, which houses a fascinating collection of snakes (both indigenous and exotic), turtles, tortoises, leguaans (iguanas) and crocodiles. Among the rarer residents are albino snakes with white bodies and red eyes.

Roggeland Country House, overlooked by the lofty Drakenstein mountains, was built in 1778 and retains the thatch-roofed, gabled gracefulness of the original; reception rooms feature high-beamed ceilings, polished yellowwood and grand fireplaces; the cooking is cordon bleu.

Franschhoek offers many fine guest lodges: **Mountain Manor** hotel and conference centre and **Swiss Farm Excelsior** (*see* p. 91) and the intimate **La Cotte Inn**.

Somerset West has the five-star **Lord Charles Hotel**, a place of elegant opulence (expanses of marble, beechwood trim, cascades of plants and lovely flower arrangements are features of the public rooms), every modern amenity and impeccable service.

If your planned overnight stay is further afield, **Goudini Spa** is a refreshing stop. A few kilometres outside Worcester, it offers rondavels and flats, swimming pools, warm baths, jacuzzis and a restaurant. Worcester has the **Cumberland Hotel**.

Ceres offers the long established **New Belmont,** representing the best of the old-style South African hostelry, and the cozy **Herberg** guest-house; Tulbagh has the **Tulbagh Hotel** and **De Oude Herberg**.

Left: *Emerald vineyards mantle the countryside around Worcester.*

7
A Day Away

Just about the whole of the region from Cape Town north through the Winelands, east across the mountains and up the western coastal belt is scenically attractive, well developed for tourism, and the visitor has a wide choice of hotels, lodges, coach and minibus excursions. Consult Captour (*see* p. 122) for guidance on the specifics. For those with their own transport, the options for day-drives and forays further afield are virtually limitless.

THE PENINSULA ★★★

The breathtaking coasts and countryside south of Cape Town are covered in a fair amount of detail between pages 45 and 67. For the independent motorist, two circular trips are especially recommended:

To **Cape Point** and back. This is the longer route, taking you in anti-clockwise progression around the Peninsula, from the city to Sea Point's Beach Road (M6) and then along the western shoreline's Victoria Drive (M6) to Hout Bay (*see* p. 55). Spend time at the charming harbour, and at the World of Birds park, and then perhaps have lunch at Kronendal, a rather lovely Cape Dutch homestead (built in 1800) on the town's main road.

Continue over Chapman's Peak (M6) (stunning views; *see* p. 56) and down past Noordhoek to Kommetjie. The turn-off, along the M65, is inland from a suburb called Sun Valley. The M65 will take you on to Scarborough and then across the southern part of the Peninsula until you reach the entrance to the Cape of Good Hope Nature Reserve (*see* p. 59), which ends at Cape Point.

PENGUIN PARADE

Parts of the coast are home to the vulnerable **Cape penguin**, commonly known as the jackass penguin for its harsh, braying call. The **jackass** is one of only two species of this flightless seabird found in SA (the other is the rare **rockhopper penguin**, which occurs only as a straggler). Among colonies accessible to visitors is that at **Boulders** near Simon's Town. The largest is on **Dassen Island**, off the western seaboard, where nearly 100,000 birds congregate.

Opposite: *The glory of Namaqualand in springtime.*

The return journey brings you down the east, or False Bay, coastline, along the M4 through Simon's Town, Fish Hoek and Muizenberg. Thereafter, follow the main highway (M3) back to the city.

The reverse (clockwise) itinerary – up the east and down the west coast – is of course just as pleasant.

The shorter circular route is a truncated version of the round trip. Head for **Hout Bay** and then, instead of carrying on along the coast, turn inland on the M63, which takes you up the exquisite Hout Bay valley to the roundabout at Constantia Nek. Here you can either bear left onto Rhodes Avenue (still the M63) to the renowned Kirstenbosch National Botanical Gardens (*see* p. 73) or continue straight on, down the Constantia valley on the M41 – a beautiful woodland route that will bring you to the Groot Constantia (*see* p. 75) turn-off on your right. The Old Cape Farm Stall is en route and worth visiting.

Groot Constantia is a place for lingering. The Cape Dutch manor house, wine cellar and museum are open for inspection; the grounds invite the stroller; both the restaurants offer fine cuisine (*see* p. 76).

Back to the city via the main M3 highway. If you didn't take the initial Kirstenbosch option – and if you have the time and energy – digress left onto the M63 (signpost Bishopscourt) and you'll see the Kirstenbosch National Botanical Gardens a short way along.

Below: *Most estates offer organized wine tours.*

THE WINELANDS ★★★

There are numerous organized coach and minibus day drives and excursions on offer from tour operators, nearly all of whom are based in Cape Town. Alternatively, one can explore on one's own, and without too much prior planning – the entire Wineland countryside is a delight to the eye and an invitation to the inquisitive mind and tastebuds. Simply wandering where the mood and moment lead will brings its rewards.

The character of the region and its principal attractions are covered between pages 79 and 101.

Among the more popular self-guided itineraries is the **Four Passes Drive**, a circular route that takes you beyond the Winelands proper, across the mountains into what is known as the **Overberg**, and then back through the beautiful fruit-growing areas of **Elgin** and **Grabouw**. Each of the passes offers superlative views.

Specifically, you follow the R310 through **Stellenbosch** (see p. 81) and over the Helshoogte pass (the name means 'steep heights'); turn right on the R45 for **Franschhoek** (see p. 89) and its pass to Theewaterskloof Dam, a large and attractive stretch of water that serves as both reservoir and playground for watersports enthusiasts. Then turn right onto the R231, cutting through the lofty Groenland

> **BIG BIRDS ON VIEW**
>
> A 20-minute drive north (N7) of Cape Town, the **West Coast Ostrich Show Ranch**, offers a fascinating glimpse into the habits and habitat of these giant birds. Guided tours cover all aspects of ostrich breeding. (One ostrich egg equals 24 hens' eggs). The skin is made into shoes, handbags and wallets. Tel: (021) 972-1955/1669.

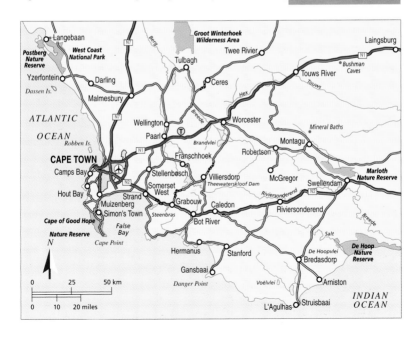

Above: *The Hex River Valley's export grapes.*

mountains via Viljoen's pass; digress to the right through **Grabouw** and take time out to see something of the apple industry.

The village has a small museum devoted to the story of the fruit; visitors are welcome at the two large packing houses, though don't just pop in unannounced: rather contact the local information officer about laid-on tours. Leave Grabouw to join the main N2 highway leading west over the magnificent **Sir Lowry's pass** past Gordon's Bay and to Cape Town via Somerset West.

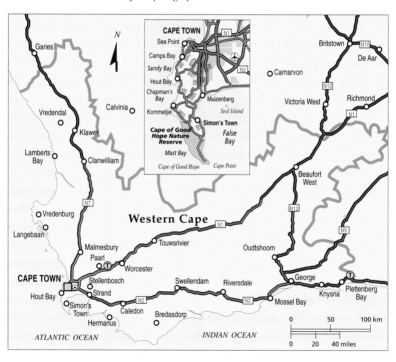

Other recommended routes include the **Boland** and **Hex River** circular drives. The former starts from **Paarl** (*see* p. 94) to follow the road to **Wellington** (*see* p. 96), **Worcester** (*see* p. 99) and the delightful little town of **Villiersdorp** before returning to Paarl via **Franschhoek** (*see* p. 89). The latter begins at **Ceres** (*see* p. 97) and heads northeast on the R46, looping southeast to join the N1 highway to **Worcester** and the **Karoo National Botanic Garden** (*see* p. 100), continuing on to **Rawsonville** and **Goudini**, known for its hot springs, and then back to **Ceres** (*see* p. 97) via the stunningly scenic Michell's Pass (*see* p. 97).

Special-interest Routes

A number of thematic itineraries have been charted, giving the visitor a balanced choice of general and special-interest destinations.

These include the **Fruit routes**, among which **Ceres** (*see* p. 97) features prominently; the Breede River and Four Passes fruit-ways are also worth exploring.

The **Cheese route** leads you to select dairy farms (some of which are also wine farms) which produce distinctive cheeses. Some wine estates also serve delicious cheese platters.

Among other specialized itineraries are the **French Huguenot Farms**, the **Arts and Crafts**, and the **Antiques** routes. Covering a wider area are the **Wreck route** along the south and west coasts, the **Crayfish** (rock lobster) route along the west coast, and the **Whale route** stretching from the Peninsula eastwards to **Hermanus** and **Walker Bay** (*see* p. 109).

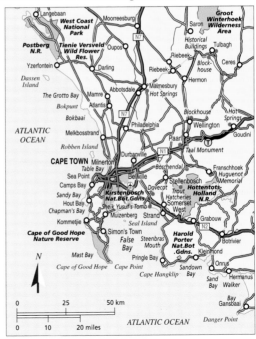

Captour at the Tourism Gateway in the city (*see* p. 122) has full information on these, as well as pamphlets and booklets that guide you to the best birdwatching spots, to the historic lighthouses, to places where you'll see fine displays of the Western Cape's unique *fynbos* and wild flowers.

WATCHING THE WHALES

From July to about November, whales can be seen sporting in the inshore waters along the coast from **St Helena Bay** to **Mossel Bay**. The best of the viewing sites though, is the stretch from **False Bay** to **Hermanus**. Whale-watchers from all over the world gather on the cliff-top above Hermanus during the season. The giant marine mammals enter the bays both to mate and, after a year-long gestation period, to calve.

Today the total southern right population visiting the country's waters is estimated at about 1600, and the number is growing at a healthy 7% a year. Other occasional sightings include the humpback whale, Bryde's whale and the killer whale.

Call the Whale Hotline tel: 0800 228-222 or the MTN Whale Crier tel: 083 212-1075.

Below: *The picturesque harbour of Gordon's Bay.*

SOUTHERN SEABOARD *

The 120km-route (75 miles) from Cape Town to the quaint seaside centre of **Hermanus** is a scenic delight.

Beyond **Somerset West** the marine drive cuts through coastal mountains to the picturesque village of **Gordon's Bay**, popular among Capetonian weekenders, upcountry holidaymakers and affluent owners of second homes. Private yachts and commercial fishing boats bob companionably together in the harbour; sunlovers make for the soft sands of Bikini and Main beaches, sporting anglers for the open sea, where fine catches of tuna and yellowtail are routinely recorded.

Deep-sea fishing boats are available for charter; pleasure cruisers and paddle-skis for hire. The small village is known for its speciality shops (hand-knitted Kei carpets are a feature), its Van Riebeeck Hotel and its three splendid holiday resorts.

Gordon's Bay is one of a number of pleasant little resort centres along this stretch of the southern coast. To the south is tranquil and unspoilt **Pringle Bay** and **Betty's Bay**. The nearby Harold Porter Botanic Garden is famed for the rich beauty of its wild flowers (the ericas are especially noteworthy) and its entrancing waterfall.

Kleinmond, at the mouth of the Palmiet River, is a holiday centre with all the amenities and a relatively wind-free climate. A variety of waterbirds congregate in their thousands on the lagoon and marshlands, and in the Kleinmond Coastal and Mountain Reserve, which is also sanctuary to more than 1500 plant species. The little village of **Botrivier**, a short distance inland, is the centre of a thriving wildflower industry, its most colourful product the salmon-pink Bot River protea.

Left: *The Old Harbour at Hermanus, once a fishing centre and now preserved as a museum.*

HERMANUS ★★★

The town, nestled between the mountains and the blue waters of **Walker Bay**, is one of the Western Cape's premier holiday spots and a magnet for whale-watchers. During the autumn and winter months these giant marine mammals, most of them southern rights, come inshore. One can't get too close to them – local conservationists make sure of that – but there are good views (through the telescope provided, but bring binoculars as well) from the high cliffs above the bay. An official 'whale crier', complete with uniform and horn, announces the arrival of these leviathans.

For the rest, Hermanus offers fine beaches, safe bathing and surfing, splendid opportunities (along the rocky coast to either side and in the placid Kleinriviersvlei lagoon) for yachtsmen, for fishermen and for divers in search of juicy crayfish (rock lobster) and *perlemoen* (abalone). Recommended is the walk along the cliff tops, and the **Rocky Mountain Way**, a scenic drive that slices through the hills. The local 18-hole golf course welcomes visitors, as does the nearby **Hamilton Russell estate**, which boasts Africa's southernmost vineyards (open Mon-Fri and Sat morning for tastings and sales).

Among the town's more ambitious tourist schemes is its **Old Harbour**, preserved in toto as a museum and a

OPEN-AIR EATING

The West Coast is famed for its seafood, freshly caught and often enjoyed in open-air, no-frills restaurants noted for their wonderfully informal sociability as well as their delicious fare. Braaing and potjiekos are features; on offer are crayfish (rock lobster), *perlemoen* (abalone), mussels, calamari (squid) and an appetizing array of line fish. Also on the menu are home-baked breads and jams. Among the best-known of these alfresco eateries are: **Die Melkbosskerm**, at the country club, Melkbosstrand; **Die Strandloper** near Langebaan; the **Breakwater Boma** at Saldanha Bay and, further north at Lambert's Bay, **Muisbosskerm**. The evenings can be chilly so wear warm clothing. The more exposed venues are wind-protected by 'skerms' (translated as rough fences).It is essential to make prior reservations to avoid disappointment.

national monument to the fisherfolk of yesteryear. The work-worn little boats on view date from the 1850s to the 1960s; scenes of the early days, when the place drew all its prosperity from the fruits of the sea, can be seen in the small stone museum building. Commercial fishermen, sporting anglers and other owners of leisure craft now use the splendid new marine complex. Some of the boats can be hired for deep-sea game fishing expeditions.

OVERBERG **

In late Victorian times the town of **Caledon**, in the Overberg ('beyond the mountain') region to the east of Cape Town, ranked as the southern hemisphere's most fashionable spa, its complex of pools, sanatorium, grand pavilion and superb **mineral springs** attracting devotees from afar. The springs, seven in all, yield more than two million litres of irradiated water a day.

Much of Caledon's splendour disappeared after the devastating fire of 1946, but imaginative efforts have been made to restore the resort to its former glory. It now boasts the splendid **De Overberger Hotel**, built on the site of the old Victorian Bath, and a growing number of visitors are 'taking the waters', drawn by the combination of hot springs, exercise, aromatherapy massage and the sense of physical well-being these create. Aerobics, horse-riding, golf, squash, bowls, tennis and walks in the lovely countryside are also part of the health-and-leisure scene.

The **Caledon Museum** is also worth visiting for its interesting Victoriana displays and its textile section.

Below: *The centuries-old, famous Houw Hoek Inn, beyond Sir Lowry's Pass.*

The quickest way to get to Caledon from Cape Town is via the N2 national highway that twists its way over Sir Lowry's pass before running eastwards through flatter terrain. If you're on an overnight visit, the De Overberger is the logical place to book into, but for a more cosy country stopover, you could try a venue in the attractive Elgin valley at the foot of the pass. The **Houw Hoek Inn**, the country's oldest licensed hotel (it's been in business since 1794), is a rustically ranch-style cluster of buildings looking out onto the duckpond and lawns over which Shetland ponies, ducks and geese wander at will. Its pub is exceptionally sociable.

THE WESTERN SEABOARD *

The Cape's west coast is very different from the southern maritime belt – dry, treeless, windy, for the most part rather bleak. But it has its attractions, and at times and in some places its beauty as well.

The journey up the shoreline from Cape Town will take you along the R27 highway, past the fast-growing centres of **Bloubergstrand** (magnificent views of Table Mountain in the distance), **Melkbosstrand** (popular among fishermen) and **Darling** (15km; 9 miles inland, but worth visiting for its cultivated lupins and the beautiful chincherinchee members of the lily family) to **Langebaan lagoon**.

For much of the way you're in sight of the sea and the drive is pleasant: it's a rather stark but often strikingly scenic coastline of jagged cliff and wide beach, heath and sandveld. On your left, opposite the tiny resort of **Yzerfontein**, you'll see **Dassen**, one of the region's larger, and in conservation terms, most important islands. Described by one scientist as among 'the naturalist's

Left: *The Greek-style village resort, Club Mykonos, on the west coast has recently been refurbished.*

EXPLORING LANGEBAAN

Visitors to Langebaan lagoon and the wider **West Coast National Park** can explore the area on one or other of the guided walks on offer. Day programmes – run by the National Parks Board from Geelbek, a restored 1860 homestead – include three short trails taking in the salt marshes, bird hides, dunes and sandveld vegetation. The programmes are advertised, and reservations made, at Langebaan Lodge. Also available are longer (three-day) educational courses and excursions, guided boat trips over the lagoon, and tours to the bird-rich islands of **Saldanha Bay**. Displays in the Lodge's foyer provide an insight into bird migration and the region's marine ecology.

Below: *Colonies of seabirds are a feature of the west coast and its islands.*
Opposite: *Churchhaven, near Langebaan lagoon.*

wonders of the world', it supports huge numbers of seabirds, serving as a breeding ground for, among others, the threatened jackass penguin (so named for its loud, braying call), nearly 100,000 that congregate on its rocky surface in February and again in September. Access is restricted, but visitors can approach by boat.

Langebaan lagoon, 120km (75 miles) north of Cape Town, is an even more impressive bird sanctuary. The 16km-long (10 miles) channel, which opens into **Saldanha Bay**, is both one of Africa's finest wetland areas and focal point of the west coast's tourism industry. Its shallow waters, the fringing mud and sand banks and the bay's islands and rocky shores, are a magnet for great concourses of summertime migrants from the Arctic and sub-Arctic regions – and for cormorants, Cape gannets, gulls, herons, plovers, knots, turnstones, sanderlings and other species.

The lagoon is the centrepiece of the fairly recently created **West Coast National Park**, which embraces the **Postberg Nature Reserve**; haven for a variety of buck species and, in springtime, venue for a breathtaking fantasia of wild flowers. Visitors stay at **Langebaan Lodge**, a pleasant hotel that also does duty as the park's headquarters and information centre. The lagoon is much favoured by the yachting and watersports fraternities.

Further up the coast, nearly 100km (62 miles) beyond **Saldanha** and best reached via the inland route, is **Lambert's Bay**, a large fishing village popular with casual holiday-makers. People come for the variety of fish and rock lobsters at **Bosduifklip**, one of the region's open-air, marvellously rough-and-ready seafood eateries. And for bird life: **Bird Island** (connected to the harbour) sustains

vast colonies of Cape gannets, cormorants, penguins, and a number of other seabirds (in fact, 150 species altogether). There are several almost-as-impressive ornithological treasure-houses in the general vicinity. **Longvlei Dam**, about 12km (7 miles) inland, is where flamingos gather in their thousands.

Inland of the Western Seaboard

For the first 150km (93 miles) the national highway (N7) leads through the **Swartland**, or 'black country' – so named for the rich darkness of its fertile soils – to the **Olifants River**. Other colours, though, are perhaps more descriptive of the countryside. Gold for the great fields of waving wheat, for instance; green for the vines and orchards and a dozen other bountiful harvests.

Malmesbury is the region's principal town. More noteworthy, perhaps, are **Citrusdal** and **Clanwilliam**, set in the lushly productive Olifants river-valley.

Citrusdal is well named: it's the centre of splendidly extensive orange groves whose first seedlings were nurtured in Jan van Riebeeck's Cape Town garden. One particular tree (now a national monument) has been bearing good fruit for the past 250 years. Washington, Naval and Valencia oranges make up the bulk of the har-

LANGEBAAN'S ANCIENT LIFE FORMS

Langebaan lagoon is an enormously rich source of **fossils**. More than 200 extinct marine and other organisms, dating back to the **Pliocene period**, have been identified to provide a fascinating insight into the region's life forms between 14 and four million years ago. At one time the lagoon also sustained vast oyster colonies, which were later destroyed by a rise in the water temperature. It is reckoned that about 30 million tons of oyster shells cover the bed of the lagoon – valuable deposits which are commercially exploited by limeworks.

vest, but the orchards also yield lemons, grapefruits and easy-to-peel hybrids. During the winter months around 6000 workers pick, sort and pack the golden crops, and the air is heavy with scent. The local cooperative lays on tours of its giant pack-house.

Clanwilliam is the headquarters of the country's rooibos tea industry. Again, visitors are welcome: tours of the estates and processing sheds are conducted during weekdays for tour groups of 15 and more. The programme includes an audio-visual presentation that covers the cultivation, grading and versatility of the leaf. The area is also noted for its gorgeous springtime blooms, at their best in the **Ramskop Nature Reserve** and **Clanwilliam Wild Flower Garden** and, further away, in the enchanting **Biewdouw** valley. The valley's farmers are commendably aware of this precious floral heritage, and move their herds of sheep and cattle to other pastures during the flowering season.

To the east of the two towns looms the towering **Cederberg**, a mountain range that takes its name from the rare and lovely Clanwilliam cedar tree. This is a vast (71,000ha; 175,441 acres) wilderness area of starkly and often strangely eroded rock formations, of caves and overhangs, peaks, ravines, cold upland streams and waterfalls, and of magnificent vistas. The highlands are criss-crossed by some 250km (155 miles) of well-defined paths, and they attract hikers, ramblers, photographers, nature-lovers and campers from all corners. For those with energy, a couple of days to spare and a liking for great, quiet spaces, the Cederberg is an ideal destination.

NAMAQUALAND ★★★

Beyond the **Olifants River** is a dry, desolate, thinly populated region of sandveld terraces (the 'raised beaches' are relics of a time before the ocean receded) known as Namaqualand – a narrow belt of increasingly arid countryside that stretches up to the Orange River and the southern dunes of the ancient Namib desert. Surface water is virtually non-existent; the terrain is harsh and seldom blessed by good rains; some places record less than 50mm (2 inches) a year.

To the casual observer, it seems that the rather arid land here cannot possibly sustain any but the toughest, least attractive life-forms.

But **Namaqualand**, incredibly, is home to more than 4000 floral species, most belonging to the daisy and mesembryanthemum groups, though others – aloes and lilies, perennial herbs, succulents – are well represented. The plants are resistant to drought, their seeds lying dormant just beneath the sandy surface during the long dry spells. Then, in that brief, promising period after the winter rains and before the onset of the searing desert breezes, they burst into glorious flower, transforming the countryside with great carpets of colourful blooms.

This wonderful springtime show is not confined to the semi-arid parts of the area. Patches of daisies and other sandveld annuals mingle with the proteas, ericas and pincushions of the Cape Floral Kingdom's *fynbos* vegetation far to the south.

The flowers are usually at their most eye-catching around mid-September, but this varies from year to year – as do the best viewing areas – according to the subtle interplay of temperature, wind and rainfall.

WATER WONDERLAND

Water-skiers rank the 18km-long (12 miles) **Clanwilliam Dam** the finest in South Africa for their sport. Moreover, it is one of the country's most attractive: the placid, ice-blue stretch of water is surrounded by vineyards and lush fields of wheat, emerald-green lucerne and vegetables, the whole picture framed by a stunning mountain backdrop. Yachtsmen, board-sailors and powerboat enthusiasts also flock to the dam. The public resort offers self-catering chalets and caravan-camping sites with excellent facilities.

Opposite: *A strangely sculpted rock formation in the rugged Cederberg.*
Left: *A springtime scene near Wuppertal.*
Overleaf: *A bird's-eye view of the fair Peninsula.*

Cape Town at a Glance

Sep and **Oct** (spring): pleasant for the crisp air, and *fynbos* in flower; **Mar** and **Apr** (autumn) for balmy, still days that have lost the scorch.

A number of direct flights from most of the world's capitals land at Cape Town **international airport**, 22km (14 miles) from the city. For more information, *see* pp 122, 123.

Entire length of the eastern peninsula serviced by excellent **rail network**, linking southern suburbs to the city. Timetables available from Tourism Gateway (TG). **Waterfront** linked to city centre by a **shuttle bus**; leaves from outside **TG**, Adderley Street. Blue-and-yellow **Rikkis**; inexpensive roving cabs, also cater for small groups who like to devise their own fun tours, tel: (021) 23-4888. Most **car-hire** firms represented.

The following is a representative but not comprehensive selection of accommodation in and around Cape Town. A full list is available from the Tourism Gateway.

City and Surrounds
Cape Swiss Hotel: Pleasant setting on the lower slopes of Table Mountain in Kloof Street, tel: (021) 423-8190, fax: 426-1795.

Capetonian Protea: Pier Place, Heerengracht, near central area and harbour, excellent seafood, tel: (021) 419-5670, fax: 419-7876
Cape Sun: City centre (Strand Street, linked to main shopping area by concourse); several restaurants (traditional Cape dishes, French cuisine, carvery), tel: (021) 488-5100, fax: 423-8875.
City Lodge – V&A: Located at gateway to the Waterfront (walking distance from city centre), tel: (021) 419-9450, fax: 419-0460.
Holiday Inn Garden Court – De Waal Drive: Close to Company's Garden, tel: (021) 465-1311, fax: 461-6648.
Holiday Inn Garden Court – Eastern Boulevard, Woodstock, linked to the city by major motorway; splendid views of mountains and harbour, tel: (021) 448-4123, fax: 447-8338.
Holiday Inn Garden Court – Greenmarket Square: Central city, overlooking charming piazza, tel: (021) 423-2040, fax: 423-3664.
Holiday Inn Garden Court – St George's Mall: Central, on pedestrian mall, tel: (021) 419-0808, fax: 419-7010.
Mount Nelson, Gardens: World-renowned elegant luxury hotel. Personal service, superb cuisine, tel: (021) 423-1000, fax: 424-7472.
Town House: On the fringes of the city centre; quietly tasteful, tel: (021) 465-7050, fax: 465-3891.

Tulbagh Protea Hotel: Quiet, located in attractive central city square; tel: (021) 421-5140, fax: 421-4648; Central reservations for all Protea Hotels 0800 11 9000.

Waterfront
Breakwater Lodge: Vibrant setting, good value, tel: (021) 406-1911, fax: 406-1070.
Victoria & Alfred Hotel: Converted historic harbour building, tel: (021) 419-6677, fax: 419-8955.
The Table Bay: The ultimate in five star luxury and comfort, excellent cuisine, superlative views over mountain or bay, in-house spa, tel: (021) 406-5000, fax: 406-5656.

Atlantic Seaboard
Ambassador Hotel and Executive Suites, Bantry Bay: Spectacularly set on water's edge, tel: (021) 439-6170, fax: 439-6336.
The Bay, Camps Bay: Splendid luxury, spectacular seaviews, tel: (021) 438-4444, fax: 438-4455.
Karos Arthur's Seat, Sea Point: Near beach, tel: (021) 434-3344, fax 434-1187.
The Peninsula All-suite Hotel, Sea Point: Overlooking Table Bay, tel: (021) 439-8888, fax: 439-8886, toll-free 0800 22 4433.
Ritz Inn, Sea Point: Short distance from the seafront; noted for revolving restaurant, tel: (021) 439-6010, fax: 434-0809, tollfree reservations 0800 11 9000.

Cape Town at a Glance

Winchester Mansions Hotel, Sea Point: Family hotel on seafront; tel: (021) 434-2351, fax: 434-0215.

Suburbs and Peninsula
City Lodge, – Mowbray Golf Park: 10 minutes' drive from city and airport, tel: (021) 685-7944, fax: 685-7997.
Vineyard Hotel, Newlands: Historic country house, tel: (021) 683-3044, fax: (021) 683-3365.
Holiday Inn Garden Court – Newlands: Close to Newlands rugby and cricket grounds, Kenilworth racecourse, tel: (021) 61-1105, fax: 64-1241.
Alphen Hotel, Constantia: 18th-century manor house, tel: (021) 794-5011, fax: 794-5710.
The Cellars-Hohenhort Country House, Constantia: Luxury in spacious grounds tel: (021) 794-2137, fax: 794-2149.
Shrimpton Manor, Muizenberg: Small and cosy, tel: (021) 788-1128, fax: 788-1129.
Lord Nelson Inn, Simon's Town: tel (021) 786-1386, fax: 786-1009.

Stellenbosch
Devon Valley Protea: Country hotel set amid the vineyards, tel: (021) 882-2012, fax: 882-2610.
D'Ouwe Werf, Church St: Small, historic and charming, tel: (0221) 887-4608, fax: 887-4626.

Stellenbosch Hotel, Dorp Street: Known for its character (some parts date back to 1743) and all-round excellence, tel: (021) 887-3644, fax: 887-3673.
Lanzerac Hotel, Lanzerac St: Gracious, historic atmosphere, tel: (021) 887-1132, fax: 887-2310.
L'Auberge Rozendal, Omega Rd, Jonkershoek: On wine farm, tel: (021) 883-8737.

Somerset West
Lord Charles Hotel, cnr Stellenbosch/ Faure Rds: One of the country's best, tel:(021) 855-1040, fax: 855-1107.

Paarl
Grande Roche, Plantasie Street: Luxury hotel set among terraced vineyards: plush, international standards. tel: (021) 863-2727, fax: 863-2220.
Mountain Shadows, off Klein Drakenstein Road: Family hospitality in tranquil setting, tel: (021) 862-3192.
Roggeland: Historic country house set in heart of Dal Josaphat Valley; excellent cuisine, tel (021) 868-2501, fax: 868-2113.

Franschhoek
La Cotte Inn, off Huguenot Road: Country style, tel: (021) 876-2081, fax: 876-2082.
Le Ballon Rouge, Reservoir Street: Stylish and upmarket, tel: (021) 876-2651.
Franschhoek Mountain Manor: tel: (021) 876-2071.

Self-catering
The choice is wide, ranging from sophisticated city apartments through houses and cottages to self-contained chalets in the heart of the countryside. Contact Captour or Holiday Booking Service, tel: (021) 24-3693

Budget
For Bed and Breakfast information, tel: (021) 683-3505, fax: (021) 683-5159.

City and Surrounds
Anatoli, Napier Street: Fine Turkish fare served in Middle Eastern surrounds, tel: (021) 419-2501.
Biesmiellah, Bo-Kaap: Cape Malay cuisine; no alcohol allowed, tel: (021) 423-0850.
Champers, Deer Park Drive: Rather formal, but friendly; French cuisine, artistic detail, tel: (021) 465-4335.
Floris Smit Huis, Church Street: International focus, tel: (021) 423-3414.
The Grill Room, Mount Nelson Hotel: Elegant, old-style service, continental cuisine, tel: (021) 483-1000.
Kaapse Tafel, Queen Victoria Street, Gardens: Cape cuisine, tel: (021) 423-1651.
La Brasserie, Holiday Inn Garden Court, St George's Mall: Varied menus, modern setting, tel: (021) 419-0808.
Maria's Greek Restaurant, Dunkley Square: Small, excellent fare, tel: (021) 461-8887.

Cape Town at a Glance

Miller's Thumb, 10b Kloof-nek Road, Tamboerskloof: Fish fare, tel: (021) 424-3838.
Aubergine, Barnet Street, Gardens: Superb service, varied menu (with emphasis on Cape and German dishes), tel: (021) 465-4909.
Rozenhof, Kloof Street, Gardens: Classic menu, fine food, tel: (021) 424-1968.

Waterfront
Teacher's Spirit of Adventure Floating Restaurant: Wine and dine while cruising the harbour, tel: (021) 419-3122.
Aldo's, Victoria Wharf: Classic Italian regional cuisine, seafood specialities, tel: (021) 421-7846.
Arlindo's Seafood Restaurant, Victoria Wharf: Mediterranean character, tel: (021) 421-6888.
Dodge City Diner, Victoria Wharf: Casual 1950s style, tel: (021) 418-1445.
Ferryman's Tavern, East Pier: Converted railway shed; brewery next door; splendid beer, tel: (021) 419-7748.
Green Dolphin, Pierhead: Seafood, pasta. Jazz nightly, tel: (021) 421-7471/5.
Hildebrand, The Pierhead: Popular lunch venue; dinner reservations essential, excellent service; Continental cuisine, tel: (021) 425-3385.
Morton's on the Wharf, Victoria Wharf: Echoes of New Orleans, with Cajun food and blackened grills; tel: (021) 418-3633.

Panama Jack's Tavern, Elliot Basin, Cape Town docks: Informal sea-food eatery, tel: (021) 447-3992.
Planet Hollywood: Theme eatery with movie memorabilia, tel: (021) 419-7827.
Quay Four: Outdoor tavern downstairs, smarter upstairs, tel: (021) 421-2088.
The Greek Fisherman, Victoria Wharf: Great calamari, tel: (021) 418-5411.
The Musselcracker, Victoria Wharf: Seafood buffet, vegetarian and Halaal specialities, tel: (021) 419-4300.
The Waterfront Café, V&A Hotel: Innovative cuisine, memorable harbour views, tel: (021) 419-6677.

Suburbs and Peninsula
Au Jardin, Vineyard Hotel, Claremont: Elegant, classic French cuisine, notable wine-list tel: (021) 683-1520.
The Beach Club, Camps Bay: Superb Mediterranean fare; friendly, relaxed atmosphere, tel: (021) 438-1213.
Blues, Camps Bay: Fine food superlatively served, varied menu, tel: (021) 438-2040/1.
Restaurant at the Bay, Bay Hotel, Camps Bay: Nouvelle cuisine, elegant atmosphere, tel: (021) 438-4444.
Europa, Sea Point: Elegant old house, seafood specialities, tel: (021) 439-2820.
La Perla, Sea Point: Seafood, Italian tel: (021) 434-2471.
Africa Café, Observatory: Ethnic dishes from throughout Africa, tel: (021) 47-9553.

The Courtyard, Vineyard Hotel, Newlands: Light lunches, tel: (021) 683-3044.
Peddlars on the Bend, Constantia: Country fare, rural surrounds, excellent value, tel: (021) 794-7747.
Buitenverwachting, Constantia: De-luxe, award-winning restaurant. Very formal, tel: (021) 794-3522.
Constantia Uitsig Restaurant, Constantia: Fine, Mediterranean Provençal cuisine, highly recommended, tel: (021) 794-4480.
The Brass Bell, Kalk Bay: Popular with the locals, overlooking the harbour, excellent seafood, tel: (021)788-5455.
Black Marlin, Miller's Point (near Simon's Town): Good seafood eating with bayside views, tel: (021) 786-1621.
Lord Nelson Inn, Simon's Town: Cozy, colonial; seafood, tel: (021) 786-1386.

Franschhoek
The Cape's 'food capital' has many fine restaurants.
Chez Michel: Good country cooking, tel: (021) 876-2671.
Haute Cabriere: Gourmet lunches, tel: (021) 876-3688
La Maison de Chamonix: tel: (021) 876-2498/2393.
La Petite Ferme: Popular venue, tel: (021) 876-3016.
Le Ballon Rouge: French-SA fusion, tel:(021) 876- 2651.
Le Quartier Français: Bistro, tel: (021) 876-2151.
Boschendal: Cape buffet; Le Pique-Nique among the pines; Le Café, tel: (021) 874-1031.

Cape Town at a Glance

Paarl

Bosman's, Grande Roche Hotel: Gourmet cuisine, rated among the country's best, tel: (021) 863-2727.

Rhebokskloof: Wine estate with three restaurants, small lake featuring black swans, tel: (021) 863-8606.

Schoongezicht Restaurant, Dal Josafat valley: Cape Dutch farmhouse; traditional Cape fare, tel: (021) 688-2616.

Somerset West

Garden Terrace, Lord Charles Hotel: Superb Cape Malay dishes, carvery and buffet, tel: (021) 855-1040.

L'Auberge du Paysan: Top, award winner for traditional French fare, smart atmosphere, tel: (024) 842-2008.

96 Winery Road; Cape, Provencal and eastern influences, tel: (021) 842-2020.

Stellenbosch

There are so many restaurants and pubs in the town and on surrounding wine farms, it is advisable to obtain the free guide to the area from Captour or the Stellenbosch Tourist Bureau and Wine Route Office (*see* p. 121).

De Akker: Hearty, pub food, tel: (021) 883-3512.

De Volkskombuis: Traditional Cape cooking, tel: (021) 887-2121.

Doornbosch: Modern, smart, specializes in Italian fare, tel: (021) 887-5079/6163.

Jan Cats: Wholesome pub fare, tel: (021) 887-3644.

Legends: Pizzas, pastas and steaks, tel: (021) 887-2313.

Lord Neethling Restaurant: Splendid Cape homestead; Cape and Continental dishes tel: (021) 883-8966.

Mamma Roma: Sociable, tel: (021) 886-6064.

O'Hagans: Traditional Irish pub and food; daily specials, tel: (021) 886-6238.

Uncle Ben's: Burgers a speciality, tel: (021) 886-5583.

TOURS AND EXCURSIONS

Balloon tours: Winelands Hot-Air Ballooning, tel: (021) 863-3192.

Canoeing in the winelands: Felix Unite River Adventures, tel: (021) 683-6433, fax: 683-6488; River Rafters, tel: (021) 712-5094, fax: 712-5241.

Coach tours around the Peninsula, winelands and West Coast:
Hylton Ross Tours, tel: (021) 438-1500, fax: 438-2919; Mother City Tours, tel: (021) 551-2580, fax 551-7281; Windward Tours, tel: (021) 790-2012, fax: 790-3633; Tailormade Tours, tel: (021) 712-9800, fax: 712-9001; Specialized Tours, tel: (021) 425-3259, fax: 425-3329.

Cycling tours and hire: Bikeabout Cycle Tours and Daytrippers, tel: (021) 531-3274; Mike Hopkins Motorcycles and Bicycles, tel: (021) 423-8461, fax: 424-5428; Rent 'n Ride, cycles and rollerblades for hire tel: (021) 434-1122.

Deep Sea Game Fishing: African Fishing Safaris, tel: (021) 438-5201; Big Game Fishing Safaris,tel: (021) 64-2203, fax 64-3837; Neptune Deep Sea Angling, tel: (021) 782-3889, fax: 782-6969.

Off-the-beaten-track Tours: Eco Explorers tel: (021) 92-9361, fax: 930-5166;

Helicopter trips over the Peninsula and Winelands: Civair, tel: (021) 419-5182, fax: 419-5183; Court Helicopters, Waterfront, tel: (021) 425-2966, fax: 425-1941; Airport, tel: 934-0560, fax: 934-0568; Sport Helicopters, tel: (021) 434-4444; Flamingo Flights, tel: (021) 790-1010, fax: 790-0300.

Steam-train trips of winelands and wildflower regions: Computicket, tel: (021) 430-8010; Union Ltd Steam-train Tours, tel: (021) 449-4391.

Horse trails on the beach or in the winelands (day and overnight trails): Dunes Racing Stables, Noordhoek, tel: (021) 789-1723; Vineyard Horse Trails, tel: (021) 981-2480, fax: 981-8509; Rozendal Horse Trails, tel: (021) 886-5794 or 082 650-5794.

Specialized tours (*see* also Coach tours): Vineyard Ventures, tel: (021) 434-8888, fax: 434-9999; Sealink, (variety of boat trips, cruises, charters), tel: (021) 425-4480.

Train trips: Blue Train reservations, tel: (021) 405-2672; Rovos Rail, long and short excursions in restored carriages, tel: (021) 421-4020.

Cape Town at a Glance

Walking Tours: Malay Quarter ((Bo-Kaap), Tasneem Tours, tel: (021) 406-1066; Table Mountain and other walks, Cape Town School of Mountaineering, tel: (021) 61-9604;

City and Surrounds
Cape Town Tourism Gateway (Captour): Visitor's information bureau, Adderlely Street (see p. 122): tel: (021) 418-5214, fax: 418-5227.
Computicket: Book for theatre, ballet, opera, cinema, concerts and sports events at booths in shopping malls, or over the telephone (give your credit card number and collect tickets at the venue). Tel: (021) 430-8010.
Farm stalls: For fresh produce and wholesome Cape fare; Old Cape Farm Stall, Constantia, tel: (021) 794-7062; Barnyard Farmstall, Tokai, tel: (021) 712-6934.
Imax (large format cinema) BMW Pavilion, V&A Waterfront, tel: (021) 419-7365.
Muizenberg Tourist Information Bureau, Atlantic Road, tel: (021) 788-1898, fax: 788-2269.
Historic Naval Dockyard Tour, Simon's Town. (021) 787-3911.
Nico-Dial-A-Seat: theatre, opera and ballet bookings, tel: (021) 421-7695.
Robben Island: for arranged visits and official tours, tel: (021) 418-5834.

Rondevlei Nature Reserve, Perth Road, Grassy Park: Variety of bird life, including pelicans, flamingos; hippos, tel: (021) 706-2404.
The Scratch Patch, semi-precious gemstones. Dido Valley, Simon's Town, tel: (021) 786-2020; V&A Waterfront, tel: (021) 419-9429.
Simon's Town Publicity Association tel: (021) 786-2436. Museum, 786-3046.
The World of Birds, Hout Bay: Largest bird park in Africa, tel: (021) 790-2730.
Tygerberg Zoo, Klipheuwel Exit off N1: Variety of animals, tel: (021) 884-4494.
V & A Waterfront Visitors Centre: tel: (021) 418-2369.

Stellenbosch
Stellenbosch Publicity Association: tel: (021) 883-3584 or 883-9633, fax: (021) 883-8017.
Stellenbosch Wine Route Office, 36 Market Street: tel: (021) 886-4310, fax: 886-4330.
The Van Ryn Brandy Cellar, Vlottenburg Road: experience the art of wine making, and cooperage tel: (021) 881-3875.

The Village Museum Complex, Ryneveld Street: tel: (021) 887-2902.
Spier Estate, on the R310: Day out for the whole family. Tel: (021) 809-1100.

Paarl
Paarl Publicity Association, cnr Main/Auret streets: tel: (021) 872-3829/4842.
Bhabhathane, Dal Josafat: Handweaving project, tel: (021) 872-9317 or 868-1394.
Le Bonheur Crocodile Farm: tel: (021) 863-1142.
Wiesenhof Game Reserve, Klapmuts Road: Animals, picnic areas, tel: (021) 875-5181.
West Coast Ostrich Show Ranch, on the N7 from Cape Town: tel: (021) 972-1955.

Hermanus
Hermanus Publicity Association tel: (0283) 22629, fax: 70-0305.
Whale Hotline: tel: 800 228-222 or 083 212-1075.

Worcester
Kleinplasie Open-air Museum: tel: (0231) 70200.
World of Snakes: tel: (0231) 26480 or 70200.

CAPE TOWN	J	F	M	A	M	J	J	A	S	O	N	D
AVERAGE TEMP. °F	70	70	69	63	58	55	54	55	57	61	64	68
AVERAGE TEMP. °C	21	21	20	17	15	13	12	13	14	16	18	20
Hours of Sun Daily	11	10	9	7	6	6	6	7	8	9	10	11
SEA TEMP. °F	59	57	55	55	54	54	54	55	55	57	57	67
SEA TEMP. °C	15	14	13	13	12	12	12	13	13	14	14	14
RAINFALL in	1	1	1	2	3	4	3	3	2	2	1	1
RAINFALL mm	14	17	19	39	74	92	70	75	39	37	15	17
Days of Rainfall	5	4	5	8	12	12	11	13	10	8	5	5

9
Travel Tips

Tourist Information

Cape Town is 1402km (871 miles) from Johannesburg, 1460km (907 miles) from Pretoria, and 1753km (1089 miles) from Durban. The region is well served by international and domestic airlines and by an excellent road system. Rail and passenger coach services connect the city with major centres. **Publicity Associations**: **Captour**, tel: (021) 418-5214 /5202. The main tourist information centre is located on the first floor of the **Tourism Gateway**, the city's tourist information office, at the junction of Heerengracht and lower Adderley Street, east of the fountain; tel: (021) 418-5214, fax: 418-5227. It is open daily from 08:30 – 19:00. Weekends: 08:30 – 17:00. Sundays: 08:30 – 12:00. P.O. Box 1403, Cape Town, 8000. Services include: accommodation, car-hire,tour advice and bookings; a range of brochures covers accommodation, eating out, shopping, special-interest routes; also a monthly *What's On* guide, street and other maps.

False Bay office: Atlantic Road, **Muizenberg**, tel: (021) 788-1898; Northern Suburbs: Shop 007, Tyger Valley Shopping Centre, **Bellville**; tel: (021) 948-4993.

The Tourism Gateway houses the regional offices of **Satour** (the South African Tourism Board), and information desks for the National Parks Board and the V&A Waterfront. It no longer takes bookings for the Table Mountain Cableway.

Entering South Africa

All visitors need passports to gain entry to South Africa. Most foreign nationals, however, are exempt from visa requirements, including citizens of the European Community, the United States, Australia, New Zealand, Japan, Austria, Brazil, Singapore, Switzerland and most southern African countries.

Health Requirements

Visitors from or passing through a yellow fever zone must be able to produce a valid International Certificate of Vaccination.

Such zones extend through most of tropical Africa and South America (air travellers in airport transit are exempt from the requirements). Note that cholera and smallpox certificates are no longer needed, and there is no screening for Aids.

What to Pack

Cape Town can be very hot in summer, cold and damp in winter. Dress is generally informal; shorts, jeans and tee-shirts the norm in summer (beachwear, though, is appropriate only at the beach, by the pool and on private property). Sunscreen is essential. 'Smart casual' wear is often required after dark at theatres and other venues, and by the more sophisticated hotels and restaurants.

Air Travel

Cape Town international airport is 22km (14 miles) from the city, accessible from the N2 national highway.
Inter-Cape operates a shuttle between the airport and central Cape Town, tel: (021) 934-0802; car rental facilities and taxis are available at – and some hotels provide courtesy transport to and from – the airport.

Road Travel

The region has an extensive and well-signposted network of national (prefix 'N'), metropolitan ('M') and regional ('R') highways. Surfaces are generally in very good condition.
Driver's licence: This must be carried at all times! Licences of neighbouring countries are valid in South Africa. So too are foreign licences provided they carry a photograph and are either printed in English or accompanied by an English-language certificate of authenticity. Alternatively, obtain an International Driving Permit before departure.

Insurance: Third Party cover is essential. Comprehensive car insurance is highly recommended. Rental firms will arrange such cover if you're hiring a car. Insurance tokens are obtainable at most points of entry for overland travellers.
Petrol: Cape Town, its suburbs, the outlying centres and main routes are well provided with fuel outlets and service stations. Many of them stay open 24 hours a day; others usually from 06:00 to 18:00. Petrol, either Super or Premium, is sold in litres; self-service is in its infancy in South Africa; pump attendants see to fuel and service needs.
Road rules and signs: In South Africa, you drive on the left; the general speed limit on major routes is 120kph (75 mph), that on secondary (rural) roads is 100kph (60 mph), and in built-up areas 60kph (35 mph) unless otherwise indicated. Keep to the left, and pass on the right on highways with many lanes. Main roads are identified by colour signs and numbers rather than by name.
Maps: Excellent regional and city maps are available from the AA, Satour and Captour and bigger bookshops. Recommended is the *Globetrotter Travel Map of Cape Town*, and those in the *Globetrotter Road Atlas of South Africa* and the *Map Studio* series.
Automobile Association: The AA of South Africa offers a wide range of services to members and members of affiliated motoring organiza-

tions. These include: assistance with breakdowns and other emergencies; insurance; car hire; accommodation reservations; touring, caravanning, camping advice; brochures and maps. Main regional office: AA House, Hammerschlag Rd, off Oswald Pirow St, Foreshore; tel: (021) 419-6914 (general, and touring information); toll-free number for breakdowns, emergency services and locksmith 0800 -010101; Mayday medical hotline, toll free 0800 033 007.

Car hire: Major, internationally-known rental companies Avis, Imperial (incorporating Hertz), Budget – maintain offices in Cape Town, at the airport and at other points throughout the wider region.
Taxis: Cape Town's cabs do not cruise the streets in search of fares (nothing like London or New York). They are found in a number of designated city ranks and at several, but by no means all, suburban railway stations. Taxi companies are listed in the *Yellow Pages*. If your journey involves anything more than a simple, cross-city hop, ask the taxi driver for an estimate of cost, and make quite sure he can locate your destination precisely.
Grab-a-Student, tel: (021) 448-7712, fax: 448-7714 employs students who need to earn extra money, and they drive you around in your hired car. The advantages are that they are familiar with the roads, one-ways and parking areas. They are usually a mine of information on history,

tourist attractions, and often speak a foreign language. (Request when booking).

There are also the so-called **black taxis** – minibuses that patrol the main thoroughfares and travel to and from the townships. They are cheap, fast (sometimes too fast), sociable, often very crowded, and will stop if you hail them, but are not recommended for tourists. Rather call **Rikki Taxis**, a quick, three-wheeler service which covers the central area; tel: (021) 423-4888.

Buses: Regular services link the city with all major suburbs. The main bus terminal is behind (to the west of) the Golden Acre complex.

Trains: Regular train services connect the city with the southern, southeastern and northeastern suburbs, but not the central and western parts of the Peninsula. The main rail terminus is on Lower Adderley Street. During the early 1990s criminals were active on some stretches of the line; security has been tightened, but it's suggested nevertheless that you seek advice (from Captour or hotel reception) before embarking on an evening trip beyond the nearer suburbs.

Accommodation

The best of the Western Cape's hotels are of an international standard but, generally, local hoteliers still have a lot to learn from their counterparts in the rest of the world.

A voluntary grading system, covering all types of accommodation, is in operation; ratings range from one to five stars.

Many of the better establishments are controlled by one or other of the large hotel chains; most offer packages, out-of-season, family rates and other inducements. The more prominent of the hotel groups are Sun International, Southern Sun/Holiday Inn, City Lodge (few frills, competitive rates), Karos and Protea, which is a management rather than proprietary enterprise, and its hotels have kept their individual yet professional characters.

Visitors have a wide choice of **guest-houses**. (Publication available from bookshops).

The outlying areas are well endowed with country getaways – restful little **lodges** tucked away in the valleys. Most of them are supremely comfortable, some highly sophisticated in terms of appointment and cuisine; all are informal and friendly.

Guest farms are ideal for the low-cost, healthy family holiday. One stays in either the farmhouse or a chalet or cottage on the property, and takes part in the life of the ranch, farm or wine estate as the case may be.

Self-catering options throughout the wider region are numerous and varied, ranging from basic holiday apartments and cottages to well-appointed, even luxurious resort-type chalets.

Bed-and-breakfast accommodation is becoming increasingly popular, and many Capetonians are making their homes available to visitors. Ask your travel agent or Captour for details.

Business Hours

Normal trading and business hours are: Mon-Fri 08:30-17:00, Sat 08:30-13:00. Most supermarkets stay open till 18:00, later on Fridays, and on Saturday afternoons and Sunday mornings. Corner cafés and suburban mini-markets stay open from early to late every day of the week. Liquor stores close at 18:30. V&A Waterfront (Victoria Wharf) shops offer night shopping.

Electricity

220/230 volts AC at 50 cycles/second; 15-amp 3-pronged (round pin) plugs. Most hotel rooms have 110 volt outlets. Not all electric shavers will fit hotel and plug points; visitors should seek advice about adaptors from a local electrical supplier.

Embassies and Consulates

Most countries have diplomatic representation in South Africa, maintaining their principal offices in Pretoria. They are listed in the *Yellow Pages* (under Consulates and Embassies) and in telephone directories (listed under the country's name).

Gambling

South Africa's gambling laws are under review. Betting on horses has always been legal and enormously popular. Until recently casinos were restricted to African 'homelands', but are gradually being established in and around most major centres.

Language

South Africa has 11 official languages; those most commonly spoken in and around Cape Town are English, Afrikaans (the home language of most Coloured people) and Xhosa (the home language of most of the the Cape's black residents).

Measurements

South Africa has adopted the metric system. A conversion chart appears on p. 126.

Medical

Visitors are responsible for their own arrangements, and are urged to take out medical insurance before departure.

PUBLIC HOLIDAYS

1 January (New Year's Day)
Good Friday and **Family Day** (Easter Monday)
21 March (Human Rights Day)
27 April (Constitution Day)
1 May (Workers' Day)
16 June (Youth Day)
9 August (National Women's Day)
24 September (Heritage Day)
16 December (Day of Reconciliation)
25 December (Christmas Day)
26 December (Day of Goodwill)

The Jewish, Islamic and Hindu communities observe their traditional holy days.

ROAD SIGNS IN AFRIKAANS

Altough often expressed also in English, some common Afrikaans words you'll come across include:
Links (left)
Regs (right)
Stad (city)
Straat (street)
Weg (road)
Rylaan (avenue)
Lughawe (airport)
Hawe (harbour)
Hou oop (keep open)
Gesluit (closed)
Gevaar (beware, hazard)
Verbode (forbidden)
Ompad (detour)
Tuin ('garden', but often used with 'wild'
e.g. **Wildtuin** – to denote a park or game reserve)
Strand (beach)
Note that, in South Africa;
Robot is a traffic light.

Private doctors are listed in the telephone directory under 'Medical Practitioners'.

Hospitalization is usually arranged through a medical practitioner, but in an emergency a visitor may telephone or go directly to the casualty department of a General (public) Hospital. Hospitals are listed under 'H' in the telephone directory.

Public hospitals tend to be rather crowded and the staff invariably overworked. Private hospitals generally offer more comfort and individual attention, but are a lot more expensive.

Aids: The incidence of HIV infection remained relatively low during the early 1990s but, much like in the rest of the world, the disease is likely to reach critical proportions before long. The risk of contracting Aids, though, is no greater in South Africa than in any other country, provided the standard and well-publicized precautions are taken.

Money Matters

The South African currency unit is the Rand, divided into 100 cents. Coins are issued in denominations of 1c, 2c, 5c, 10c, 20c, 50c, R1, R2 and R5; while notes are available in denominations of R10, R20, R50 ,R100 and R200. Coinage designs have been subject to change, and some denominations circulate in two forms. Beware of the similarity between the old 20c piece and the R2 coin.

Currency exchange: Foreign money can easily be converted into rands at banks and also through such authorized dealers as Thomas Cook and American Express.

Banks: Normal banking hours are 09:00 to 15:30 on weekdays and 08:30 or 09:00 to 11:00 on Saturdays. There are banking and exchange facilities at Cape Town international airport. Traveller's cheques may be cashed at any bank and at many hotels and shops.

Credit cards: Most hotels, restaurants, shops, car rental companies and tour operators accept international credit cards (American Express, Bank of America, Visa, Diners Club, Mastercard). Note that you cannot buy petrol with a credit card; most banks issue special 'Petrocards'.

Value Added Tax (VAT): see Shopping.

Tipping: Provided you receive satisfactory service, it is usual to tip porters, waiters and waitresses, taxi drivers, room attendants and golf caddies. Tipping the petrol attendant is optional. Gratuities for quantifiable services (waiters, taxi drivers) should amount to at least 10% of the cost of the service; for non-quantifiable services of a minor nature (porterage, for example), it is customary to proffer between R2 and R5.

Service charges: Hotels may not by law levy a charge for general services (though there is often a telephone service loading). Restaurants may levy such a charge; few do so.

Newspapers

The major English-language dailies are the *Cape Times, Business Day* (morning) and *The Cape Argus* (afternoon). The latter brings out special Saturday and Sunday editions. Also available are the national weekly newspapers the *Mail and Guardian, The Sunday Times* and the *Sunday Independent,* and Afrikaans papers. Foreign newspapers are sold by selected newsagents and in some hotels.

Photography

Most international film brands and sizes are readily available in Cape Town's photographic shops and department stores; processing is quick (same-day; one-hour at some outlets).

Postal Services

Most post offices are open from 08:00 to 16:30 weekdays and 08:00 to 12:00 noon Sat. An international priority mail service is available. Stamps also available at CNA and some cafès and supermarkets.

Safety and Security

Do not walk alone at night; avoid deserted and poorer areas unless you're with a conducted group. Don't carry large sums of cash around with you; don't leave valuables in your room (use the hotel's security box).

Shopping

The full range of necessities and luxuries is available in Cape Town. A 14% **Value Added Tax** (VAT) is levied on all sales of goods and services. This is usually reflected in the quoted price. Foreign visitors can claim back VAT paid on items that are to be taken out of the country (retain the tax invoice for this purpose).

Local products of particular interest to tourists include gold, diamond and semi-precious stone jewellery; copperware; leather (including crocodile and ostrich skin); suede goods; items made from karakul wool, mohair, ostrich feathers; ceramics; curios and African handicrafts.

Telecommunications

The telephone system is fully automatic; and one can dial direct to most parts of the world. The telephone directory lists dialling codes. Both local and long-distance calls are metred. Dial 1023 for directory queries. Fax transmission facilities are widely available. Public call boxes accept either coins or Telkom phone cards.

Time

Throughout the year, South African Standard Time is two hours ahead of Greenwich Mean (or Universal Standard) Time, one hour ahead of European Winter Time, and seven hours ahead of US Eastern Standard Winter Time.

CONVERSION CHART		
FROM	**TO**	**MULTIPLY BY**
Millimetres	inches	0.0394
Metres	yards	1.0936
Metres	feet	3.281
Kilometres	miles	0.621
Kilometres square	Square miles	0.386
Hectares	acres	2.471
Litres	pints	1.760
Kilograms	pounds	2.205
Tonnes	tons	0.984
To convert Celsius to Fahrenheit: x 9 ÷ 5 + 32		

INDEX